ESSENTIAL MESSAGES FROM GOD'S SERVANTS

masterWork

Lessons from

THE MURDER OF JESUS

by John MacArthur

LIFE ESSENTIALS

by Tony Evans

SPRING *2007*

Ross H. McLaren

Editor in Chief

Gena Rogers

Editor

Carolyn B. Gregory

Copy Editor

David Wilson

Graphic Designer

Melissa Finn

Lead Technical Specialist

John McClendon

Lead Adult Ministry Specialist

David Apple and Mic Morrow

Adult Ministry Specialists

Send questions/comments to

Editor, *MasterWork*

One LifeWay Plaza

Nashville, TN 37234-0175

Or make comments on the web at

www.lifeway.com

Management Personnel

Ron Brown and Larry Dry,

Managing Directors

Leadership and Adult Publishing

Bret Robbe, *Director*

Leadership and Adult Publishing

David Francis, *Director*

Sunday School

Bill Craig, *Director*

Leadership and Adult Ministry

Gary Hauk, *Director Publishing*

LifeWay Church Resources

ACKNOWLEDGMENTS.—We believe the Bible has God for its author; salvation for its end; and truth, without any mixture of error, for its matter and that all Scripture is totally true and trustworthy. The 2000 statement of *The Baptist Faith and Message* is our doctrinal guideline.

Lessons by John MacArthur are condensed from *The Murder of Jesus* (Nashville: Thomas Nelson, Inc., 2000, 2004). Used by permission of Thomas Nelson, Inc.

Lessons by Tony Evans are condensed from *Life Essentials* (Chicago: Moody Press, 2003). Used by permission of Moody Press.

Unless otherwise indicated, all Scripture quotations in the lessons from *The Murder of Jesus* are from *The New King James Version.* © 1979, 1980, 1982, 1984 by Thomas Nelson, Inc., Used by permission. Unless otherwise indicated, all Scripture quotations in the lessons from *Life Essentials* are from the *New American Standard Bible.* © The Lockman Foundation, 1960, 1962, 1963, 1968, 1971, 1972, 1973, 1975, 1977, 1995. Used by permission. Quotations in the "How to Become a Christian" article or those marked HCSB are taken from the *Holman Christian Standard Bible®,* copyright © 1999, 2000, 2001, 2002 by Holman Bible Publishers. Used by permission. This translation is available in a Holman Bible and can be ordered through LifeWay Christian Stores. Passages marked NASB are from the *New American Standard Bible.* © The Lockman Foundation, 1960, 1962, 1963, 1968, 1971, 1972, 1973, 1975, 1977, 1995. Used by permission. Quotations marked NIV are from the Holy Bible, *New International Version,* copyright © 1973, 1978, 1984 by International Bible Society. This translation is available in a Holman Bible and can be ordered through Lifeway Christian Stores.

MasterWork: Essential Messages from God's Servants (ISSN 1542-703X) is published quarterly by LifeWay Christian Resources of the Southern Baptist Convention, One LifeWay Plaza, Nashville, Tennessee 37234; Thom Rainer, President. © Copyright 2006 LifeWay Christian Resources of the Southern Baptist Convention. All rights reserved. Single subscription to individual address, $26.35 per year. If you need help with an order, WRITE LifeWay Church Resources Customer Service, One LifeWay Plaza, Nashville, Tennessee 37234-0113; For subscriptions, FAX (615) 251-5818 or EMAIL *subscribe@lifeway.com.* For bulk shipments mailed quarterly to one address, FAX (615) 251-5933 or EMAIL *CustomerService@lifeway.com.* Order ONLINE at *www.lifeway.com.* Mail address changes to: *MasterWork,* One LifeWay Plaza, Nashville, TN 37234-0113.

Printed in the United States of America.

Cover photo credit: Getty Images

table of Contents

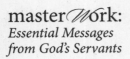

master*Work:*
*Essential Messages
from God's Servants*

• Designed for developing and maturing believers who desire to go deeper into the spiritual truths of God's Word.

• Ideal for many types of Bible study groups.

• A continuing series from leading Christian authors and their key messages.

• Based on LifeWay's well-known, interactive model for daily Bible study.

• The interspersed interactive personal learning activities **in bold type** are written by the writer identified on the Study Theme unit page.

• Teaching plans follow each lesson to help facilitators guide learners through lessons.

• Published quarterly.

ABOUT THE WRITERS

John MacArthur, one of today's foremost Bible teachers, is the author of numerous best-selling books that have touched millions of lives. He is pastor-teacher of Grace Community Church in Sun Valley, California, and president of The Master's College and Seminary. He is also president of Grace to You, the ministry that produces the internationally syndicated radio program *Grace to You* and a host of print, audio, and Internet resources—all featuring John's popular, verse-by-verse teaching. He also authored the notes in *The MacArthur Study Bible,* which has been awarded the Gold Medallion and has sold more than 500,000 copies. John and his wife, Patricia, have four grown children and twelve grandchildren.

For more details about John MacArthur and all his Bible-teaching resources, contact Grace to You at 800-55-GRACE or *www.gty.org.*

AMY SUMMERS wrote the personal learning activities and teaching plans for this quarter. Amy is an experienced writer for LifeWay Bible Study curriculum, a mother, and a Sunday School leader from Arden, North Carolina. She is a graduate of Baylor University and Southwestern Baptist Theological Seminary (M.R.E.).

ABOUT THIS STUDY

Read Isaiah 53:4-11 and answer the following:

What **did Jesus endure?**_____

Why **did Jesus endure such suffering?**_____

Who **was in control of all that happened to Jesus?**

_____

How **will you respond to this wonder of divine justice worked through human injustice?**_____

The Murder of Jesus

It's easy to look at the cross and conclude that this was the worst miscarriage of human justice in the history of the world. And it was. It was an evil act, perpetrated by the hands of wicked men.

But that is not the *full* story. The crucifixion of Christ was also the greatest act of divine justice ever carried out. It was done in full accord with "the determined purpose and foreknowledge of God" (Acts 2:23)—and for the highest of purposes: The death of Christ secured the salvation of untold numbers and opened the way for God to forgive sin without compromising His own perfectly holy standard.

Christ was no mere victim of unjust men when He hung on the cross. Though murdered unjustly and illegally by men whose intentions were only evil, Christ died willingly, becoming an atonement for the sins of the very ones who killed Him. It was the greatest sacrifice ever made; the purest act of love ever carried out; and ultimately an infinitely higher act of divine justice than all the human *in*justice it represented.

My aim in these lessons is to examine the biblical account of Christ's arrest, trials, and crucifixion—and in doing so to try to unfold the rich redemptive significance of our Lord's work on the cross.

John MacArthur

Kiss of the Traitor

day One

A Mob Approaches

Judas was approaching with a large armed mob sent by the chief priests and elders from the temple.

Read Matthew 26:47 printed in the margin. How did Matthew identify Judas?
❑ **The betrayer**   ❑ **The one we suspected**
❑ **One of the Twelve**

Judas seemed like a typical disciple. He had obviously never given the other disciples any reason to distrust him, because they were all caught completely off guard when he approached with the mob seeking to capture Jesus. The disciples' sense of shock is clearly conveyed in the exclamation Matthew employs to describe Judas's sudden appearance on the scene: *"Behold, Judas . . . ."*

Judas's facade of faithfulness to Christ makes his treachery particularly heinous. The insidiousness of a close friend who pretended loyalty and love for Christ while betraying Him is far worse than if Christ had been handed over by someone known to be an enemy.

Read Psalm 55:12-14. What caused David great pain?

_____

Why is betrayal by a friend far worse than harm inflicted by an enemy?

_____

Judas's action is shown to be even more shameful by the fact that he brought a large mob armed with swords and clubs. They were prepared

"While He was still speaking, behold, Judas, one of the twelve, came up accompanied by a large crowd with swords and clubs, who came from the chief priests and elders of the people" (Matt. 26:47, NASB).

for violence. They were set to do bodily harm to Christ and the disciples, if necessary. And this was not an impromptu mob of citizens but a hand-selected band of thugs carefully organized by the chief priests and elders.

Luke says the mob included members of the temple guard ("captains of the temple"—Luke 22:52). These were security officers who acted as policemen in the temple grounds and also had limited powers (sanctioned even by Rome) to arrest people for violations of the Jewish law (see John 7:32). On at least one prior occasion, the chief priests had ordered the captains of the temple to arrest Jesus, but when they heard Him teach, they were so confounded by the way He spoke with authority that they came back stunned and empty-handed (John 7:45–46).

John notes that the mob also included a detachment of Roman soldiers (John 18:3). Since the arrest of Jesus had been orchestrated by the Sanhedrin, they must have been the ones who requested the soldiers to participate in taking Jesus. Obviously they planned to try Him on capital charges, and since only Rome had authority to carry out the death penalty, it was necessary to have a contingent of soldiers involved at the time of the arrest. A garrison of Roman soldiers was permanently stationed at the Antonio Fortress, adjacent to the temple mount. These soldiers were no doubt sent from there.

None of the Gospels gives a numerical estimate of the size of the mob, but Matthew, Mark, and Luke all agree that it was a great multitude (see Mark 14:43; Luke 22:47). Depending on the size of the detachment of soldiers, the crowd could easily have numbered in the hundreds. The fact that the chief priests sent such a large crowd to make the arrest indicates the degree to which they were frightened of Jesus' power. Many times before this they had sought to arrest Him or silence Him, and their schemes had always been foiled. Jesus Himself called attention to their absurd and cowardly tactic of sending an armed multitude to arrest Him in the middle of the night. "Have you come out, as against a robber, with swords and clubs to take Me? I sat daily with you, teaching in the temple, and you did not seize Me" (Matt. 26:55). Such a large group was clearly overkill.

It was also unnecessary. They would face no resistance from Jesus.

Read Matthew 26:53. What could Jesus have done if He had not been willing to be arrested?

If it were not now His time in the perfect plan of God, He could easily have escaped even from such a large mob, as Jesus pointed out to Peter (v. 53).

The Evil Deed Is Done

"Immediately Judas went to Jesus and said, 'Hail, Rabbi!' and kissed Him" (Matt. 26:49, NASB).

It had been a few hours at most since Judas left the Upper Room. It already was dark outside when he left, and by the time he arrived with the band of armed men it could not have been much later than midnight. Obviously he had gone directly from the Upper Room to the chief priests. Ever since they had paid him the blood money, he had been seeking an "opportunity to betray Him to them in the absence of the multitude" (Luke 22:6). Now, just in case, the conspirators decided to bring with them a multitude of their own. It obviously would have taken some time to round up such a crowd. But the readiness with which they were able to assemble so many temple guards, armed soldiers, and others shows their level of determination. Who knows what they had told the Roman authorities in order to get an immediate detachment of troops like this? Clearly they had falsely made Jesus out to be a serious threat to Roman interests.

Read John 18:1-3. Why did Judas take the mob to the Garden of Gethsemane?

_____

Perhaps that evening's trip to Gethsemane had been planned and discussed ahead of time among the disciples. Or maybe it was such a well-established habit that Judas simply knew where Jesus would go after supper. In any case, Judas must have been fairly certain Jesus would be there to have brought such a large crowd along with him. As far as the conspirators were concerned, it was an ideal place to arrest Jesus without arousing the notice of the multitudes.

Judas previously had arranged a signal by which he would identify Jesus for his fellow conspirators. Judas may have also feared that one of the disciples would surrender to the authorities in Jesus' place, pretending to be Him in order to spare His life. After all, just hours before in the Upper Room, Judas had listened while each of the other disciples had professed his willingness to go to prison or die for Christ (John 13:37; Luke 22:33). Therefore, to be certain that they could distinguish Jesus from the others, the conspirators had set up their prearranged signal. Judas had told them, "Whomever I kiss, He is the One; seize Him" (Matt. 26:48). The kiss in that culture was a sign of respect and homage as well as affection. Slaves kissed the feet of their masters as the utmost sign of respect. Disciples sometimes kissed the hem of their teacher's garment as a token of reverence and deep devotion. It was common to kiss someone on the hand as a gesture of respect and honor. But a kiss on the face, especially with an embrace, signified personal friendship and affection. The gesture was reserved for the closest of friends, so a disciple would not ordinarily embrace and kiss his teacher unless the teacher first offered the kiss.

The word Matthew employs to describe Judas's kiss is *kataphileo,* which means "to kiss earnestly, intensively, or repeatedly."

Read Luke 7:37-38 where *kataphileo* is also used. What does this term for kiss signify to you?

_____

As if it weren't enough for Judas to betray Jesus, in doing so he pretended the utmost affection, making his act even more despicable. Under Satan's control, Judas evidently knew no shame. He could have chosen any signal for identifying Christ to his fellow conspirators. He deliberately chose one that compounded his own guilt with the most diabolical kind of hypocrisy. He seems to have deliberately drawn out his kissing in order to detain Jesus as long as possible, to be sure that the soldiers had time to apprehend Him.

In what ways have you betrayed Jesus?_____

_____

_____

"Friend, Why Have You Come?"

Jesus' reply to Judas's false display of affection conveys a tone of sadness, but no malice or hostility.

> " 'Friend,' Jesus asked him, 'why have you come?' Then they came up, took hold of Jesus, and arrested Him" (Matt. 26:50, HCSB).

As you read Matthew 26:50, printed in the margin, underline what Jesus called Judas.
How do you feel about that and why? _____

_____

There is a note of restraint and possibly aloofness in the expression. Christ did not employ the normal word for "friend." It was not *philos,* the word He used in the Upper Room when He told the disciples, "You are My friends if you do whatever I command you. No longer do I call you servants, for a servant does not know what his master is doing; but I have called you friends" (John 15:14–15). When He addressed Judas He used the word *hetairos,* meaning "comrade" or "companion." Nonetheless, there is an irony in the fact that when Peter, a true friend, tried to impede Jesus' advance to the cross, Jesus addressed him as "Satan" (Matt. 16:22–23). But here Judas—a willing tool of Satan, indwelt and controlled by the prince of darkness himself—hands Jesus over to those who would crucify Him, and Jesus addresses him only as "comrade."

Jesus asks, "Why have you come?" not because He did not know. He wanted Judas to face up to—and the other disciples to recognize— what an evil thing Judas was doing. Luke records that He said, "Judas, are you betraying the Son of Man with a kiss?" (Luke 22:48). Even at this late hour, when Judas's heart was so obviously hardened against Christ, there is still an obvious tenderness in the way Jesus dealt with him. He uttered no invective; He did not speak harshly to Judas or call him names that would have been perfectly fitting, such as *villain, infidel, traitor,* or *fool.* Instead, He addressed him as a comrade, called him by his name, and gently asked questions that would have smitten the conscience of anyone who was not utterly hardened. Judas's perfidy, set against the backdrop of Jesus' tenderness, looks all the more wicked.

Describe a time you received undeserved tenderness from Jesus.

_____

Pause right now to thank Him for being your gentle Friend.

But Judas was not deterred. He did not break stride. With bold-faced treachery, he handed Jesus over to His executioners, still pretending affection yet nurturing the most diabolical hatred in his heart.

Later, Judas would have deep regret over what he had done (Matt. 27:4–5). But even then his regret was devoid of any true repentance. Having sold himself to Satan for thirty pieces of silver, he had already doomed himself to an eternity apart from the Holy One whom he so callously betrayed. It would have been better for him if he had not been born (26:24).

> "The Son of Man is to go, just as it is written of Him; but woe to that man by whom the Son of Man is betrayed! It would have been good for that man if he had not been born" (Matt. 26:24, NASB).

day Four

A Slaughter Is Averted

Having heard all Jesus' talk of betrayal and His predictions about His arrest and crucifixion, the disciples did not go into the garden unarmed. Earlier that evening in the Upper Room, when Jesus was informing them that one of them would betray Him, Luke records an interesting exchange.

Read Luke 22:36–38, printed in the margin.

Christ was cautioning them about the impending violence. A horrific act of violence was about to be perpetrated, and Jesus was warning them of a spiritual battle they were about to face. He certainly was not telling them to arm themselves with fleshly weapons.

> "And He said to them, 'But now, whoever has a money belt is to take it along, likewise also a bag, and whoever has no sword is to sell his coat and buy one. For I tell you that this which is written must be fulfilled in Me, 'AND HE WAS NUMBERED WITH TRANSGRESSORS'; for that which refers to Me has its fulfillment.' They said, 'Lord, look, here are two swords.' And He said to them, 'It is enough' " (Luke 22:36-38, NASB).

Read 2 Corinthians 10:3-4. Why don't Jesus' followers need fleshly weapons?

But the disciples mistakenly assumed that He literally meant for them to go and purchase swords. So they had taken inventory and found they already had two swords among them. Jesus' ambiguous reply ("It is enough") probably meant "enough of such talk." They may have thought He meant two swords were sufficient. Of course two weapons of that sort would be practically useless against an armed mob that included so many Roman soldiers.

There was nothing unusual about Galilean fishermen carrying swords. These were long double-edged knives or daggers rather than full-length fighting swords. They were carried in a leather sheath strapped to the belt, and they had numerous practical uses other than violence against other people.

When the disciples realized that Jesus was about to be taken by force, they asked, "Lord, shall we strike with the sword?" (Luke 22:49). They were undoubtedly emboldened by something only John reports. When the attackers announced that they were seeking Jesus of Nazareth, "Jesus said to them, 'I am He.' . . . Now when He said to them, 'I am He,' they drew back and fell to the ground" (John 18:5–6). Such a display of supernatural power may have spurred the disciples' thinking that Jesus planned to destroy His attackers supernaturally. So they asked Him if they should use their weapons.

Except for Peter. He saw no point in thinking or talking at this point. John tells us, "Simon Peter, having a sword, drew it and struck the high priest's servant, and cut off his right ear. The servant's name was Malchus" (v. 10).

Malchus was in all likelihood a high-ranking servant of the high priest, because he was apparently positioned at the front of the mob, an easy target for Peter. Peter was undoubtedly slashing at his neck or literally trying to split his skull, but Malchus flinched and Peter's blow glanced off the side of his head, severing the ear.

Jesus severely rebuked Peter: "Put your sword into the sheath" (John 18:11). Christ had no need of fleshly power to defend Him. He had already made that point in a graphic way when His mere words caused His attackers to stagger and fall to the ground. He continued His rebuke of Peter, "Do you think that I cannot now pray to My Father, and He will provide Me with more than twelve legions of angels?" (Matt. 26:53). A legion was comprised of 6,000 soldiers. Twelve angelic legions would be 72,000 angels. In the Old Testament—when Sennacherib's armies threatened Jerusalem—a single angel slew 185,000 Assyrian troops in one night (2 Kings 19:35). So the military might of 72,000 angels would be quite imposing! If Christ had intended to be rescued from this armed mob, He certainly would not have needed Peter's sword.

But Jesus reminded Peter He had a higher purpose: "How then could the Scriptures be fulfilled, that it must happen thus?" (Matt. 26:54).

Read the following passages and note how Scripture was fulfilled that night in the garden.

Psalm 2:1-2 _____

Psalm 41:9 _____

Isaiah 53:7-8 _____

If angels rescued Him at this point, His atoning work could not be accomplished. "Shall I not drink the cup which My Father has given Me?" (John 18:11). Once again, Peter's rash intervention was a fleshly impediment to the plan of God.

Malchus's severed ear was apparently still dangling from the side of his head. In a remarkable display of Jesus' power, "He touched his ear and healed him" (Luke 22:51).

Read Luke's account of this incident in Luke 22:47-54. What do you find remarkable about this miracle?

_____

Perhaps the most remarkable fact is that the miracle was virtually ignored by the mob. They carried on with their evil business as if nothing out of the ordinary had happened (v. 54). The healing of Malchus's ear had no more effect on their hearts than the powerful force that had knocked them to the ground a few moments before. Even a miraculous display of God's power would not deter them from the evil goal they had set their hearts on.

The Disciples Flee

" 'Awake, O sword, against My Shepherd, and against the man, My Associate,' declares the LORD of hosts. 'Strike the Shepherd that the sheep may be scattered' " (Zech. 13:7, NASB).

It was at this point that Jesus said to the mob, "Have you come out, as against a robber, with swords and clubs to take Me? I sat daily with you, teaching in the temple, and you did not seize Me" (Matt. 26:55). The cowardly way they came out against Jesus in the dead of night was proof that they knew they had no legitimate grounds for arresting Him. He was involved in no clandestine insurrection. He had done His teaching publicly and in broad daylight, usually on the temple grounds, in full view of everyone. If there had been lawful grounds for arresting Him, He could have been taken into custody on almost any day during that previous week. The Sanhedrin knew, of course, that such a public arrest could stir the crowd. That is why they had conspired to arrest Jesus secretly. But by saying this, Jesus exposed their subterfuge to the Roman soldiers who probably knew nothing about the Jewish leaders' real motives.

Jesus added, "But all this was done, that the Scriptures of the prophets might be fulfilled" (v. 56). Thus Christ again sounds the refrain that is the constant theme of all four Gospel accounts of the crucifixion. Despite their hostility to Christ, the men who arrested Him were fulfilling His sovereign purposes perfectly. Their attempts to destroy Him were only achieving *His* chosen ends, fulfilling a plan that was established before time began. His Word and His will would be fulfilled no matter how fiercely the powers of darkness sought to destroy Him.

Christ had now been betrayed into the hands of His enemies. There was nothing the disciples could do to stop it. Utter despair set in. They could draw no comfort from Jesus' reassuring words. Fear began to overwhelm them.

According to Matthew 26:56, what did the disciples do when they focused on the circumstances rather than God's purposes?

_____

Remember that even their desertion occurred so the Scriptures might be fulfilled. They were acting precisely as Jesus said they would. If they reflected on these things at all, they must have realized that not one disaster had befallen them that He had not previously warned them about. The disciples literally scattered, rather than fleeing as a group. Nothing is said about where the other disciples went—but they apparently went into hiding. Peter and John secretly followed the mob to the high priest's house (John 18:15).

In fairness to the disciples, we should note that they all would indeed have been arrested or worse if they had stayed in the garden. That fact is evident from Jesus' plea to the arresting officers, recorded in John's account: "If you seek Me, let these go their way" (John 18:8). Probably when they heard Jesus say those words, they seized the moment and fled without hesitation. They all deserted their Master.

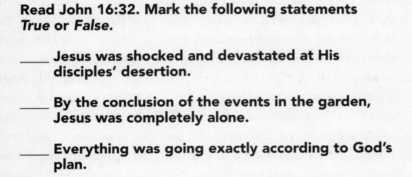

Read John 16:32. Mark the following statements
***True* or *False*.**

____ **Jesus was shocked and devastated at His disciples' desertion.**

____ **By the conclusion of the events in the garden, Jesus was completely alone.**

____ **Everything was going exactly according to God's plan.**

The divine work of redemption continued on schedule, despite the opposition of His enemies—and even despite the abandonment of His friends.

To the Leader:

Each teaching plan has two create interest options. The first option is geared toward those classes who prefer a discussion format. The second option usually requires a little more creativity or involvement on the part of the participants. Regardless of whether you use one of these options or your own idea, be sure to begin your lesson with a "hook" that catches participants' interest so they are ready to learn and grow.

Before the Session

1. Set up dominos so they will fall in a progressive chain.
2. Print out the NIV, HCSB and *The Message* translations of Luke 22:38 (translations can be copied from *www.biblegateway.com*).

During the Session

1. Challenge participants to name instances of injustice served by human courts. Ask: *Was Jesus' death an instance of justice or injustice? Explain.* OR Ask participants to indicate if they are wearing, or often wear, jewelry in the shape of a cross. Ask if they are proclaiming humanity's injustice or God's divine justice when they wear that cross. FOR EITHER OPTION Encourage participants to state the Who, What, When, Where, and Why of Jesus' crucifixion using their own recall and the introductory material on pages 4-5. Read the "How" question in the introduction and state that is the ultimate question participants need to evaluate throughout the course of this 7-week study.

2. Draw attention to the dominos and ask what will start them falling. Declare that a chain of events begins with one action. Direct participants who have headings in their Bibles to state the events that occurred in Matthew 26:1-46. Declare that all the dominos were in place. Judas's kiss of betrayal was the push that began the chain of events leading to the crucifixion. Remind participants that God was in ultimate control of pushing that first domino. (Option: for a visual effect, push the first domino so the others fall down.) Direct half the class to combine the facts detailed in Matthew 26:47-56 and Luke 22:47-53 to describe the events of Judas's betrayal. Instruct the other half to do the same with Mark 14:43-50 and John 18:1-11. Request groups share the chain of events that occurred in their passages.

3. Invite volunteers to read John 6:71 and Mark 14:10. Ask why participants think the Gospel writers stressed Judas's status as one of the twelve apostles. Discuss the second activity of Day 1. Discuss who

Judas brought with him to the garden and why Dr. MacArthur declared that was both overkill and unnecessary.

4. Discuss the first activity of Day 2. Lead a discussion with questions such as: *What did Judas do when he got to the garden? What signals do you think Judas could have used to point out Jesus? What made Judas's prearranged signal so despicable? What do you think Judas felt as he kissed Jesus? What do you think was going through the other apostles' minds? What do you think Jesus felt?* Discuss the first activity of Day 3. Ask: *How does Jesus' demeanor toward Judas encourage and challenge you? Why did Jesus ask Judas why he had come? How was Jesus' question answered in Matthew 26:50?* Ask someone to read the last paragraph of Day 3. Point out that although Judas's betrayal was prophesied, Dr. MacArthur says Judas doomed himself. Tell the class you will look at this in more depth in Week 3.

5. Invite someone to read Luke 22:35-38. Ask what it sounds like Jesus was encouraging His followers to do. Distribute the copies of the various translations of Luke 22:38 and ask how those translations help participants better understand this passage. Request two volunteers to read aloud John 18:10-11 and Matthew 26:52-54. Ask: *Do you think Jesus regarded Peter's action as legitimate self-defense or illegally attempted murder? Why?* Explain that Jesus doesn't forbid defending ourselves and our loved ones, but in this instance He was insisting His apostles submit to the governing authorities, even though the authorities were acting unjustly. Ask if participants think Peter was actually insulting Jesus with this violent act and why. Inquire: *What was Peter's purpose at this point? What was Jesus' purpose?* Discuss the last two activities of Day 4.

6. Use the material in Day 5 to contrast how Jesus conducted His ministry with how the authorities conducted Jesus' arrest. Explore how even the authorities' unlawful conduct achieved God's purposes. Discuss the first activity of Day 5. Ask: *Can we judge the disciples too harshly? Why or why not?* Discuss the final activity.

7. Ask: *How do we betray or abandon Jesus today? How can we guard against betraying or abandoning our Lord?* Read Hebrews 10:38-39. Encourage participants to live by faith in this One who died for them and to never shrink back from loving and serving Him. Close in prayer.

The Kangaroo Court of the High Priest

day One

Jesus Is Brought Before Annas

"So the Roman cohort and the commander and the officers of the Jews, arrested Jesus and bound Him, and led Him to Annas first; for he was father-in-law of Caiaphas, who was high priest that year" (John 18:12-13, NASB).

Jesus was taken from Gethsemane directly to Annas, the former high priest, who still wielded the power of the high priest's office (John 18:13).

Annas was one of the most powerful men in Jerusalem. He had served as high priest twenty years before this (A.D. 7–14), and for all practical purposes, he had controlled the high priest's office ever since. Five of his sons had already succeeded him as high priest, and now his son-in-law, Caiaphas, had the title. Annas thus managed to control the high priesthood through his sons and son-in-law until the end of his life. As the real power behind the office, he also retained use of the title high priest (see Luke 3:2).

Annas and family had managed to turn the high priesthood into an incredibly profitable business, and they had amassed enormous wealth through it. They did this chiefly by collecting license fees and commissions from the brokers who changed money and sold sacrificial animals on the temple grounds. The entire business was crooked. Both the money-changers and the animal merchants were renowned for their dishonesty and greed. Since Annas controlled a monopoly on the whole enterprise, the merchants who worked for him could charge exorbitant rates—especially during the seasons of the feasts when the city was filled with pilgrims. Of course Annas himself took a hefty portion of the profits. Thus Annas and his sons had grown wealthy at the expense of people who came to worship God.

Annas administered this power through his sons, who regularly collected the high priest's cut of profits from those shady businesses. Annas functioned very much like a modern organized crime boss. No wonder Christ twice purged the temple.

Read the following Scriptures and note what Jesus declared Annas had done to the temple.

John 2:13-16 _____

Mark 11:15-18 _____

How did Annas and the religious leaders respond to Jesus' declaration?

_____

No wonder Annas was so determined to eliminate Jesus. Jesus had repeatedly been a threat to Annas's business interests.

The fact that those who arrested Jesus first brought Him to Annas proves that Annas himself was the ultimate power behind the plot to kill Jesus. He ultimately had to authorize the deed, and without his sanction the evil plot never would have gone forward. Also, the fact that the conspirators took Him to Annas before they went to Caiaphas reveals the true nature of Caiaphas's high priesthood. Caiaphas was virtually a puppet, under his father-in-law's control.

The hearing at Annas's house was evidently held for one purpose: to trump up a specific charge against Jesus. The plan was for Annas to listen to Jesus give an account of His teaching, and then Annas would decide what kind of charge to file. He had several options at his disposal. He could charge Jesus with blasphemy, a crime punishable by death under Jewish law. But the Romans, who must authorize and carry out all executions, rarely approved of the death penalty for blasphemy. For that reason Annas might also look for a way to charge Jesus with sedition or insurrection. While Jesus was taken before Annas, Caiaphas would have time to gather the Sanhedrin at his house for the impromptu trial (Matt. 26:57).

John records that Annas "asked Jesus about His disciples and His doctrine" (John 18:19). In effect, Jesus was being arraigned (brought before a court to answer charges), even though He had not yet been indicted (formally charged with a specific offense). This was completely out of order and contrary to every standard of fair jurisprudence. Moreover, Annas was in effect trying to get Jesus to implicate Himself—and that was also contrary to the principles of justice that were supposed to govern the Sanhedrin.

But Jesus' reply subtly exposed the illegality of Annas's line of questioning: "I spoke openly to the world. I always taught in synagogues and in the temple, where the Jews always meet, and in secret I have said nothing. Why do you ask Me? Ask those who have heard Me what I said to them. Indeed they know what I said" (John 18:20–21). Jesus was not being impertinent. He had no legal obligation to testify against Himself, particularly before any charges were filed against Him. Annas was supposed to state the charges against Jesus before he could cross-examine Him in a hearing of this sort. Since no specific charges had been brought against Him, it was not Jesus' obligation to supply Annas with information he might later employ to incriminate Him. Annas, of course, knew this.

Nonetheless, "when He had said these things, one of the officers who stood by struck Jesus with the palm of his hand, saying, 'Do You answer the high priest like that?'" (v. 22). The officer's action was probably meant to cover the high priest's embarrassment. It may also have been a deliberate attempt to rankle Jesus, to try to goad Him into an angry retort that could be used against Him.

> **Read John 18:22-23. Circle the word that best describes Jesus' response to this insult.**
>
> **Defensive   Antagonistic   Composed   Intimidated**

Jesus retained His composure perfectly. If Jesus had spoken blasphemy or tried to foment revolution, it was His accusers' responsibility to give a detailed account and proof of His wrongdoing. If they had no knowledge of any crimes He could be charged with, they had no right to hold Him, much less strike Him.

Annas was clearly embarrassed by Jesus' response. Christ had exposed the high priest's ruse without giving him any information that would help in the trumping up of charges. Exasperated and still unable to find anything he could charge Jesus with, Annas finally had Him bound and sent Him to Caiaphas's house, where members of the Sanhedrin were already assembled for the trial.

"Those who had seized Jesus led Him away to Caiaphas, the high priest, where the scribes and the elders were gathered together" (Matt. 26:57, NASB).

Solicitation of False Testimony

Matthew writes, "Now the chief priests, the elders, and all the council sought false testimony against Jesus to put Him to death, but found none. Even though many false witnesses came forward, they found none" (Matt. 26:59–60).

It was not the business of the council to solicit anyone's testimony. They were supposed to be acting in the capacity of impartial judges, not prosecuting attorneys. By openly soliciting damaging testimony against Jesus, they forfeited any perception of impartiality. But they probably believed that if their conspiracy against Jesus did not succeed now, it would never succeed. So they were desperate. They were determined to press the issue against Jesus until they found some reasonably credible complaint against Him—even if it meant destroying any vestige of legitimacy that might have been left in their illegal hearing.

According to God's law in Deuteronomy 19:16-19, what should have been done to the false witnesses who sought the death penalty for Jesus?

The phrase "even though many false witnesses came forward, they found none" means that many people came forward who were willing to bear false witness against Jesus, but none were found credible enough to sustain a charge against Him. According to Mark, the false witnesses contradicted one another: "Their testimonies did not agree" (Mark 14:56). They couldn't even find liars who were clever enough to fabricate a tale that agreed with the lies of others.

Finally two false witnesses came forward and said, "This fellow said, 'I am able to destroy the temple of God and to build it in three days'" (Matt. 26:60–61). Mark's account sheds even more light on what these false witnesses were claiming: "We heard Him say, 'I will destroy this temple made with hands, and within three days I will build another made without hands' " (Mark 14:58). Mark further adds, "But not even then did their testimony agree" (v. 59). The details of their stories still didn't quite jibe—but there were enough similarities in what they said to give their testimony a veneer of credibility. One witness apparently claimed he had heard Christ say if the temple were torn down, He would be able to rebuild it in three days (Matt. 26:61). The other claimed what He actually said was that He *would* destroy the temple and rebuild a new temple made without hands (Mark 14:58).

They both were obviously referring to a statement Jesus had made early in His ministry, after He cleansed the temple the first time.

Read John's account of what really happened in John 2:18–21.

The incident actually took place at Passover in the first year of Jesus' public ministry—three years to the day before this trial at Caiaphas's house. Most of Jesus' hearers on that occasion wrongly assumed that He was speaking of the destruction of the actual temple. His meaning was deliberately ambiguous, and only after the resurrection did the disciples fully understand that the saying was a reference to the temple of His body (v. 21). But most of the crowd assumed He was speaking about the Jerusalem temple (v. 20). The two witnesses at Caiaphas's house had evidently both been present that day three years before, and they had not forgotten the incident, even though neither was able to give a precise account of what Jesus really claimed. The inconsistency in their testimony shows how badly Jesus' words were misunderstood by the people who originally heard Him.

Read John 8:43-47. Why did so many people not understand what they heard Jesus say?

_____

Pause to pray, asking God to give you spiritual ears to truly hear, understand, and respond to His Word.

But the testimony of those two witnesses nonetheless served Caiaphas's purposes. The testimony could be twisted to suggest that Jesus was advocating the total overthrow of the Jewish religion (by replacing the current temple with another). Furthermore, the Sanhedrin could charge Him with high blasphemy for claiming that He could rebuild the temple by miraculous means ("without hands"—Mark 14:58). After all, Herod's temple had been under construction for forty-six years (John 2:20), and although it was not yet completely finished, it was already one of the most spectacular edifices in the world. So Jesus' claim probably seemed arrogant in the extreme to anyone who assumed He was speaking about destroying and rebuilding Herod's temple. Therefore it was this claim that Caiaphas focused on. He asked Jesus, "Do You answer nothing? What is it these men testify against You?" (Matt. 26:62).

day Three

A Desperate Attempt to Get Jesus to Incriminate Himself

Since there were obvious discrepancies in the stories told by the witnesses, their testimony should have been automatically disallowed and the case against Jesus dismissed. But the Sanhedrin was obviously in no mood for that. They had already secretly determined to eliminate the threat they imagined Jesus posed to their power, and to do that, they needed credible evidence against Him. Now they seemed to have it— or at least these witnesses' testimony could be spun into something akin to proof that He was guilty of blasphemy. And so "the high priest arose and said to Him, 'Do You answer nothing? What is it these men testify against You?' " (Matt. 26:62).

Read Matthew 26:63a. How did Jesus respond to Caiaphas's challenge?

_____

It is easy to picture Him looking directly into Caiaphas's eyes with steely calm. He had no obligation to testify against Himself. And just as He had done previously with Annas, He made that point with Caiaphas in a dramatic way—by simply declining to testify against Himself. Centuries before, the prophet had foretold that very silence: "He was oppressed and He was afflicted, yet He opened not His mouth; He was led as a lamb to the slaughter, and as a sheep before its shearers is silent, so He opened not His mouth" (Isa. 53:7).

Finally in frustration, Caiaphas charged Jesus with an oath: "I put You under oath by the living God: Tell us if You are the Christ, the Son of God!" (Matt. 26:63). Obviously Caiaphas was familiar with Jesus' claims.

Read the following passages. Draw a line from the reference to the claim Jesus made about Himself.

Matthew 16:20	**God is My Father;** **I am equal with God.**
John 4:25-26	**I am the Messiah.**
John 5:18	**I am the Son of God (Man).**
John 9:35-37	**I am the Christ.**

Claiming to be God certainly would have been sufficient grounds for charging any ordinary man with blasphemy, and blasphemy was a capital crime under Moses' law ("Whoever blasphemes the name of the LORD shall surely be put to death"—Lev. 24:16.)

But Caiaphas still needed credible testimony to prove that Jesus had made such claims, and all he had was hearsay. The testimony of the two witnesses was also flawed. It would have to do, unless better evidence could be found. But before moving on, Caiaphas first placed Jesus under oath and demanded that He tell them whether He was Christ, the Son of God.

Jesus gave him precisely what he hoped for. He replied, "It is as you said. Nevertheless, I say to you, hereafter you will see the Son of Man sitting at the right hand of the Power, and coming on the clouds of heaven" (Matt. 26:64).

Read Mark 14:61-62. What two important words did Mark include with Jesus' answer?

_____ _____

"I am" was the proper name by which God revealed Himself to Moses (Ex. 3:13–14)—and thus provided personal testimony from the accused in support of the Sanhedrin's accusation that He claimed to be God. The promise of His coming on the clouds of heaven was another clear declaration of His Messiahship, an unmistakable reference to the well-known Messianic prophecy in Daniel 7:13–14.

It was all Caiaphas needed to hear.

A Predetermined Verdict

Matthew 26:65–66 says, "Then the high priest tore his clothes, saying, 'He has spoken blasphemy! What further need do we have of witnesses? Look, now you have heard His blasphemy! What do you think?'" The tearing of Caiaphas's clothes was supposed to signify his utter shock and outrage over an alleged act of open blasphemy. Tearing one's clothes was an expression of extreme grief and shock from the most ancient biblical times (see Gen. 37:34; Num. 14:6; 2 Sam. 1:11).

Read Leviticus 21:10. What is ironic about the high priest tearing his clothes in this instance?

_____

While Caiaphas was theatrically feigning indignation over Jesus' supposed act of blasphemy, he himself was actually committing a rather serious act of sacrilege, profaning the high priest's office in a way Scripture expressly forbids.

Caiaphas's artificial outrage reflected no genuine concern for the holiness of God's name. He must have been secretly overjoyed to hear Jesus say something he could accuse Him with. The exaggerated gesture of tearing his clothes would have barely disguised the glee on his face over the fact that he was finally able to get Jesus to make a statement that had the semblance of blasphemy—or would have if Jesus had been a mere man.

"I was watching in the night visions, and behold, One like the Son of Man, coming with the clouds of heaven! He came to the Ancient of Days, and they brought Him near before Him. Then to Him was given dominion and glory and a kingdom, that all peoples, nations, and languages should serve Him. His dominion is an everlasting dominion, which shall not pass away, and His kingdom the one which shall not be destroyed" (Dan. 7:13-14).

Read John 5:31-39. Identify the four witnesses that provided valid testimony Jesus was not a mere man.
Verse 33: _____
Verse 36: _____
Verse 37: _____
Verse 39: _____

As the high priest tore his clothes, he said, "What further need do we have of witnesses? Look, now you have heard His blasphemy!" (Matt. 26:65). He now had the "evidence" he needed, and to his absolute delight there was no need for any testimony from witnesses to confirm it. As far as he was concerned, Christ had blasphemed openly before the entire council. They all were witnesses against Him. His condemnation was now a done deal. The high priest immediately asked for a verdict from the council: "What do you think?"

They dutifully answered, "He is deserving of death" (v. 66). And thus the council rendered a summary verdict: "They all condemned Him to be deserving of death" (Mark 14:64). It was the verdict they had agreed upon long before they ever heard His case.

No one was permitted to speak in His defense. No voice of caution was raised at any point in the trial. No plea for mercy was entertained. None of the evidence that supported His claims was ever considered. Jesus was simply railroaded by the high priest's kangaroo court into a guilty verdict that had been arranged and agreed on long before He ever came to trial.

day *Five*

Ruthless Cruelty

Finally having accomplished the evil goal they had so long sought, the members of the Sanhedrin began to vent their satanic hatred of Jesus openly.

Read Matthew 26:67-68 and Luke 22:63-64. List the cruel actions taken against Jesus.

_____

Luke adds that there were "many other things they blasphemously spoke against Him" (Luke 22:65). Ironically, blasphemy was the very crime they had accused Him of, but they themselves were the ones who were guilty of it.

According to 1 Peter 2:23, when Jesus was insulted,

He did not _____.

When He suffered, He did not _____

_____.

Christ bore all such abuse with a quiet and majestic grace that is quite remarkable. He would soon be bearing others' sins; meanwhile, He also patiently suffered their hateful abuse.

Isaiah's prophecy, written at least seven hundred years earlier, perfectly described this moment. "He is despised and rejected by men, a Man of sorrows and acquainted with grief. And we hid, as it were, our faces from Him; He was despised, and we did not esteem Him" (Isa. 53:3). Isaiah thus prophetically foretold the whole world's sinful apathy toward Jesus Christ. No one came to His defense. No one spoke in His favor. He was left to bear His affliction all alone.

And thus Christ was unjustly condemned to die. His trial before the Sanhedrin had gone exactly according to Annas's and Caiaphas's evil plan. At the same time, the plan of God was right on schedule as well.

In what ways have you not esteemed Jesus?
❏ **I've been apathetic or complacent about His sacrifice.**
❏ **I've not spoken up for Him.**
❏ **I've not trusted Him.**
❏ **I've refused to bear my cross for Him.**

Other: _____

_____

leader Guide

To the Leader:

Sometimes your most effective teaching will occur when you are silent and allow the Holy Spirit to speak through others in your class. Pray for wisdom to know when and what to speak in your group times and when to remain silent.

Before the Session

Search "kangaroo court" at *www.wikipedia.org* to obtain a definition and description of this phrase.

During the Session

1. Ask: *Have you ever been in a court of law or situation where you felt unfairly treated? What did you do?* OR Encourage the class to state what they know about kangaroos. Ask why participants think Dr. MacArthur used the term *kangaroo court* to describe Jesus' trial. Explain the term *kangaroo court*. Declare today you will see injustice done as Jesus is bounced from one place to another and many leaps are taken in the legal system. FOR EITHER OPTION Declare that today's lesson offers a dual challenge: (1) To grow in our love for Christ by gaining a deeper appreciation of what He endured for our sake, and (2) to learn how to conduct ourselves when we are treated unfairly.

2. Invite someone to read John 18:12-13,19-23. Ask who was striving to be in control of this situation. Use the material in Day 1 to give a profile of Annas. Ask what Annas questioned Jesus about and why. Explain Annas was hoping the number and activities of Jesus' disciples and the content of His teaching would reveal subversion and rebellion. Discuss how Jesus revealed He was in control of the situation.

3. Ask someone to read John 18:24. Explain that in that culture it was typical for adult children to build homes next to their parents and between the homes would be a courtyard. So when Jesus was sent to Caiaphas, He most likely walked across this shared courtyard where Peter and John were (see John 18:15-18). Request a volunteer read Matthew 26:57-61. Ask what kind of testimony the Sanhedrin was looking for and for what purpose. Ask why they had to seek false testimony. Discuss the first activity of Day 2. Describe the accusations that were finally similar enough that the Sanhedrin felt they could use them to charge Jesus. Ask why the court would consider Jesus' claim to rebuild the temple to be sedition and blasphemy.

Request that someone read John 2:18-21. Ask what Jesus really meant by this claim. Discuss the second activity of Day 2. Lead the class to explore ways church attendees today can be so concerned about their religion that they either miss or reject the Messiah. Discuss how people can make certain they don't miss the truth when Jesus speaks it.

4. Read Matthew 26:62. Discuss the first activity of Day 3. Read Isaiah 53:7. Ask: *Do you think Jesus' silence frustrated Caiaphas? Why?* Request someone read aloud Matthew 27:63b-64. Complete the third activity of Day 3. Ask: *Why do you think Jesus didn't remain silent this time? Why did He tell them exactly what they wanted to hear? How can we know when to keep silent and when to speak up when our faith is on trial?* Request someone read aloud Mark 13:11.

5. Ask someone to read aloud Matthew 26:65-66. Evaluate why the high priest thought Jesus' statement was blasphemy and why it actually was not blasphemous. Discuss the second activity of Day 4. [Answers: John the Baptist; Jesus' miracles; God Himself; Scripture.] Ask someone to read John 5:40-44. Ask why the leaders wouldn't accept these reliable testimonies about Jesus. Inquire: *What did these men who had disregarded truth all night decide Jesus deserved for telling the truth? When do you think they decided this verdict? What evidences of justice or injustice have you observed in Jesus' trial so far?*

6. Discuss the first two activities of Day 5. Ask how Jesus was able to bear such abuse with such grace. Point out that 1 Peter 2:23 says Jesus had committed Himself to God. State that Jesus' mistreatment fulfilled Isaiah's prophecy. Ask someone to read Isaiah 53:3. Lead the class to state ways believers do not esteem Jesus. Encourage them to name ways they can esteem Jesus. Read 1 Peter 2:21 and declare one way believers esteem Jesus is to follow His example. Invite participants to share what they have learned from Jesus' example about how to respond when under trial. Discuss how participants can apply what they've learned to situations at work, church, home, or the courtroom.

7. Invite volunteers to share how today's lesson has led them to grow in love for Christ and how they have gained a deeper appreciation for His sacrifice. Close in prayer.

Crucifixion Morning

day One

The Strategizing of the Sanhedrin

The Sanhedrin needed a careful strategy for pursuing their case against Jesus.

Read John 18:31. What barrier did the Sanhedrin face in carrying out their death penalty against Jesus?

_____

A few years prior to this, Rome had rescinded the Jewish leaders' right to carry out the death penalty on their own. All capital punishment had to be approved and implemented by Roman authorities. The only exception was if a Gentile defiled the temple by traversing beyond the court of the Gentiles, he could be stoned on the spot. Sometimes over-zealous Jews would also stone people caught in the act of a capital crime (see John 8:3–11). The history of that era reveals that sometimes for the sake of political expediency Rome would turn a blind eye to such stonings—especially when they were carried out by people at the grass roots level (see Acts 7:54–60). But such tolerance would not have been extended to official verdicts rendered by the Sanhedrin. As the only Jewish court recognized and authorized by Rome, they were expected to abide by Roman policies limiting their power.

Furthermore, the authority of the Sanhedrin was confined to religious matters, and therefore relatively few of the cases they heard involved capital crimes. In extreme cases they might be able to gain Roman approval for enacting the death penalty against a particularly unruly blasphemer. But obviously the Romans (who were committed to their own mythical brand of polytheism) were not eager to incite Jewish enthusiasm for having heretics put to death.

If the Sanhedrin intended to ask Rome to execute the death penalty against Jesus, they would have to present the case against Him in a compelling way. The believability of their case against Jesus was severely compromised by the way the trial had been conducted so quickly and under cover of darkness.

How did Jesus' middle-of-the-night trial illustrate the truth of John 1:5 (printed in the margin)?

_____

> "The Light shines in the darkness, and the darkness did not comprehend it" (John 1:5, NASB).

> "That light shines in the darkness, but the darkness did not overcome it" (John 1:5, HCSB).

That may be why during the early hours of the morning (probably around 3 a.m. or 4 a.m.), the council decided to adjourn until later that morning. No doubt all were exhausted anyway. The recess would give council members time for a couple of hours' sleep, and the court could be officially reconvened in the daylight hours to render a formal verdict, in keeping with the required procedure for such cases. This way if anyone questioned the justice of the way the Sanhedrin had tried Christ, they could claim that their final verdict had been reached in full daylight.

According to Luke 22:53, what power was God allowing to reign in the hours surrounding Jesus' death?

> "Then Jesus said . . . 'but this hour and the power of darkness are yours' " (Luke 22:52,53 , NASB).

Angelic   **Demonic**   **Fear**   **Darkness**

day Two

One More Time in the Morning

They wasted no time. Luke reports that the Sanhedrin reconvened their council and brought Jesus in for their final hearing of His case "as soon as it was day" (Luke 22:66). Matthew describes the same meeting: "When morning came, all the chief priests and elders of the people plotted against Jesus to put Him to death" (Matt. 27:1).

The council subjected Christ once more to the same line of questioning Caiaphas had used the night before.

Read Luke's description of the hearing in Luke 22:66–71.

The council wanted Jesus to say _____

so that _____

They wanted Jesus to state plainly whether He was the Messiah. Having solicited many witnesses against Him, they were nonetheless unable to prove that He had ever publicly declared (in so many words) that He was the Christ.

Jesus' reply exposed the council's prejudice. If He claimed to be the Messiah, they would not believe the claim, nor would they give any serious consideration to any proofs He might bring forth. They had already seen and heard about many of the amazing proofs of His divine power. In fact, one of His greatest miracles—the raising of Lazarus—was what finally sealed their determination to kill Him (John 11:53).

Furthermore, as He pointed out, *He* had already questioned *them* about His messianic credentials, and they had refused to answer.

Read Matthew 13:14-15. Why wouldn't the leaders believe what Jesus told them?

_____

Read Luke 20:1-8. Why wouldn't the leaders answer what Jesus asked?

_____

If they could not answer the evidence that showed He was the Messiah, they ought to let Him go. But it was quite clear that they had no intention of doing either. Jesus was being railroaded; this was no legitimate trial.

But even though they did not now believe His claims, He solemnly assured them that the time would come when the Son of Man would sit on the right hand of the power of God. He was implying that the tables would one day be turned and He would sit in judgment of them.

His reply didn't quite give them what they wanted, however, so they pressed further: "Are You then the Son of God?" This time He replied simply, "You rightly say that I am" (Luke 22:70).

That was just what they wanted. Now they had Him on record, in broad daylight, claiming to be the Son of God. As He had just pointed out, whether that claim was true or not made no difference whatsoever to them. Though He had given ample evidence throughout His ministry to substantiate the claim—and some of these men had even seen that evidence with their own eyes—they were not the least bit interested in either establishing or disproving the validity of His claim; all they wanted to do now was get Him on the cross as quickly as possible. In the end, it meant they crucified Him for telling the truth.

As soon as Jesus claimed to be the Son of God, the trial was immediately brought to a close. "What further testimony do we need?" (v. 71). As had happened the night before, He was offered no opportunity to call witnesses in His defense. None of the evidence establishing the veracity of His claim was permitted. Evidence was irrelevant as far as these men were concerned. They had actually reached their guilty verdict beforehand. Christ's testimony gave them the appearance of legitimacy they needed. As far as they were concerned, all "further testimony" would be superfluous and counterproductive. They now were eager to move ahead with the execution of their sentence.

Read Matthew 27:1-2. What was the next step in their plan?
❑ **Hang Jesus immediately before the crowds were aware of what was happening.**
❑ **Take Jesus to the Roman governor to obtain permission to execute Him.**
❑ **Smuggle Jesus out of town and execute Him quietly.**

Judas's Suicide

At this point Matthew recounts Judas's earthly demise.

Read Matthew's account in Matthew 27:3–5.

We are not told where Judas was while Jesus was on trial. At the very least, it appears he was present at the conclusion of the Sanhedrin's final daylight hearing because Matthew says he *saw* that Christ had been condemned. Perhaps as Judas saw Jesus bound and led away to Pilate, the full enormity of his sin finally dawned on him. The sight of Jesus being so mistreated because of his betrayal was more than even Judas could handle. At that moment, Judas may have begun to realize for the first time the magnitude of his own sinful foolishness. He had sold the Son of God for a handful of money.

Read 1 John 1:1-2. Describe privileges Judas experienced as one of the twelve apostles.

_____

_____

No one ever sinned against so much light and so much privilege. No one ever betrayed so innocent a victim. No one ever maintained such a hard heart for so long in the presence of so much compassionate goodness. Remember, Judas had received all the same tokens of divine loving-kindness from Christ as the other disciples in his three years with the Master. But all those privileges had never impacted Judas's heart in the least. For three years he resisted and rejected all the truth he heard from Jesus. He hardened his heart against it, and he secretly grew to despise the sinless Son of God. Yet throughout those years he was such an expert in the art of hypocrisy that he managed to conceal his true character from everyone except Jesus.

"And Satan entered into Judas who was called Iscariot, belonging to the number of the twelve" (Luke 22:3 , NASB).

"So when He had dipped the morsel, He took and gave it to Judas, the son of Simon Iscariot. After the morsel, Satan then entered into him" (John 13:26b-27 , NASB).

Read John 6:70-71. Earlier in His ministry, Jesus referred to Judas as _____.

In the end, Judas happily sold all his spiritual advantages—including Christ Himself—to the highest bidder. The evil of his heart defies comprehension. No wonder Jesus called him a devil. No wonder Satan had such easy access to Judas's heart (John 13:27; Luke 22:3).

But even Judas could not escape the horrifying pain of his own guilt. The time finally came when even a heart so severely hardened and a conscience so badly seared could not cushion his soul from the sense of guilt he will bear throughout eternity.

As soon as Judas saw Jesus bound and led away, he was smitten with regret. It was not true repentance, but merely remorse. (Though the *King James Version* says Judas "repented himself," the word used is not the normal Greek word for repentance, *metanoeo,* but another word that merely signifies deep regret, *metamelomai.*) Judas was beginning to realize the bitter consequences of sin, and he hated those consequences; but he never reached the point where he hated the sin itself.

Why was Judas suddenly filled with regret when he saw that Jesus had been condemned? He may have thought when he betrayed Him that Jesus would escape arrest as He had done repeatedly before. Or perhaps Judas assumed Jesus would be able to clear Himself of any charges brought against Him. After all, He was truly innocent of any wrongdoing. And Judas had never seen Christ *fail* in any circumstances. Judas may have actually hoped Jesus would escape or be vindicated. It would be the perfect scenario. Judas would still have his thirty pieces of silver. Jesus would be no worse off for the experience. The hypocritical priests would simply be out thirty pieces of silver. Using that sort of rationale, Judas may have convinced himself that his betrayal of Jesus was no great thing and would have no serious or lasting consequences—especially if Jesus really was the true Messiah.

When have you tried to fool yourself that a sin was no big deal?

_____

What was the result? _____

day Four

Repent or Regret?

Now the sight of Christ condemned caused Judas to see for the first time the true enormity of his guilt. And it was more than he could bear.

Judas desperately wanted to escape the consequences of what he had done. Notice what he did in his effort to escape his guilt.

State the action Judas took in:

Matthew 27:3 _____

Matthew 27:4 _____

By human standards, these might seem rather impressive evidences of a kind of repentance. *First, he offered restitution.* He took the thirty pieces of silver back to the Sanhedrin and futilely begged them to take it back. He may have done this while they were still assembled at the end of Jesus' final hearing, immediately after Christ had been led away to Pilate. The money was all Judas had wanted before; now he was suddenly desperate to get rid of it because it was the physical reminder of the guilt that pained him so much. It had suddenly become like a live coal in his hands.

Read John 12:3-6. What sin appears to be prevalent in Judas's life?

Immorality   Hatred   Monetary Greed   Rage

Second, Judas offered a confession. Judas verbally confessed his guilt. He acknowledged that he had sinned; he also affirmed Jesus' innocence. He made no excuses for his action but freely admitted his wrong.

Those measures at first glance may appear to have taken him a long way toward repentance, but he still fell far short. It's true that he confessed that he had sinned, but he did not confess to God and seek true forgiveness. There was evidently no more love for Christ in his heart when he brought the money back to the Sanhedrin than when they gave him the money in the first place. The only thing that had changed was that he now felt the repercussions of his sin powerfully, and he wanted no part of his sin's *consequences.* Like so many who profess repentance today, Judas mostly just wanted to get rid of the pain his guilt caused him. The constant torment of his own conscience pangs was too much for him, and he wanted relief.

"For the love of money is a root of all sorts of evil, and some by longing for it have wandered away from the faith and pierced themselves with many griefs" (1 Tim. 6:10 , NASB).

Read 1 Timothy 6:10, printed in the margin. How does Judas's example serve as a sobering warning to believers today?

_____

Judas would receive no sympathy or support from his fellow conspirators. Their response to his confession was in effect sheer mockery: "And they said, 'What is that to us? You see to it!'" (Matt. 27:4). The callousness of their reply is astonishing. Judas plainly admitted to them that he had betrayed innocent blood. The fact that this meant nothing to them reveals how purely evil their intentions were from the very beginning. They were going to crucify Jesus with the full knowledge of His innocence.

Judas could not get them to take the money back, so he threw it into the temple and left. It was a final act of spite, designed to make them own the silver coins that had become the token of Judas's guilt.

Deuteronomy 27:25 says, "Cursed is the one who takes a bribe to slay an innocent person." Judas must have superstitiously associated the physical coins themselves with the curse, and he may have hoped to rid himself of the curse by ridding himself of the money. At the very least, he wanted to bring the same curse on his fellow conspirators. By throwing the money and leaving quickly, he left them no choice but to take the money back.

Judas, utterly friendless, hopeless, and disconsolate under the weight of his own guilt, then sealed his self-destruction forever with an act of suicide.

Perhaps Judas thought by killing himself he could finally get relief from his guilt. The opposite is true. By killing himself he bound himself to his guilt forever. Judas of all people ought to have known this, for he had repeatedly heard Jesus teach about hell—how it is a place of eternal torment, unquenchable fire, and weeping and gnashing of teeth that goes on day and night forever (Matt. 8:12; 13:42, 50; 22:13; 24:51; 25:30; Luke 13:28; Mark 9:43–48). In hell the pain of guilt and conscience pangs are eternally intensified—eating away at the soul like a worm that never is satisfied and never dies.

The full circumstances of Judas's suicide may be gleaned by comparing Matthew's account with Acts 1:18–19. Combining Luke's and Matthew's accounts, we can piece together what happened. Judas hanged himself on a weak branch of a tree—perhaps a limb overhanging a cliff or some sharp, jagged rocks in the potter's field. The limb must have broken, and Judas fell headlong onto the rocks, causing the horrible mutilation to his body Luke describes in Acts 1.

The Sanctimony of the Temple Authorities

The chief priests seemed to share Judas's superstitious attitude toward the blood money. Although Judas had managed to force them to be responsible for it, they had no desire to possess the money, nor were they willing to put it back into the temple treasury.

Read Matthew's account in Matthew 27:6–10.

What did the chief priests choose to do with the money?

_____

Matthew's reference to Jeremiah is actually an allusion to Zechariah 11:12–13: "So they weighed out for my wages thirty pieces of silver. And the LORD said to me, 'Throw it to the potter'—that princely price they set on me. So I took the thirty pieces of silver and threw them into the house of the LORD for the potter." Zechariah thus prefigured Judas's actions with uncanny accuracy. (Matthew's attribution to "Jeremiah" reflects the common way the Hebrew canon was divided into three sections: law, writings, and prophets. Just as the poetic writings were sometimes referred to collectively as "the psalms" after the first book in that part of the canon—see Luke 24:44—the prophetic writings were sometimes called "Jeremiah," after the first book in the prophetic part of the Hebrew canon.)

Matthew and Luke both mention that the field had become well known as "the Field of Blood." It was evidently a familiar place by the time the Gospels were written, about thirty years after the crucifixion. On the day Judas died there, however, it was known as "the potter's field." It was probably a vacant lot attached to a potter's business. The temple authorities bought the field after Judas died in it with the money he returned to them. They then converted the property into a cemetery for "strangers"— most likely Gentiles or outcasts.

The transaction had the appearance of an act of charity, but in reality it was rife with the grossest hypocrisy. Up to this point in their dealings with Jesus, the Sanhedrin had shown little concern for legal propriety. They had violated virtually every principle of justice in order to obtain a guilty verdict against Jesus. They had taken money from the temple treasury in order to bribe Judas to betray his Master. But on this question of whether they could place the bribe money back into the temple treasury, they suddenly began to show scruples.

The priests condemned themselves when they admitted that the silver pieces were "blood money." They were virtually confessing that the money was (in the words of Deut. 27:25) "a bribe to slay an innocent person." In stark contrast to Judas, these men seemed to feel no pangs of conscience whatsoever for the evil deed they were doing. "What is that to us?" they mockingly replied to Judas.

> **Read Matthew 23:25-28. Earlier Jesus had rebuked the Jewish leaders for: (choose one)**
> ❏ **Not washing their dishes properly**
> ❏ **Not properly caring for their ancestors' graves**
> ❏ **Caring more about outer appearances than inner purity**

The members of the Sanhedrin who condemned Christ epitomized the gross hypocrisy He had always opposed. They sanctimoniously refused to put blood money into the temple treasury in broad daylight, but they had no compunctions about secretly *paying* blood money from the treasury to Judas. They weren't concerned about their own awful guilt; they were concerned only about how they appeared to others. They had no time to consider Jesus' innocence ("What is that to us?")—they were too busy trying to make it appear that He deserved death. As long as they could cloak their evil conspiracy with an illusion of legitimacy, they were perfectly content to pursue their course of sin. They would do everything in their power to make Jesus appear guilty and themselves appear righteous— even though they knew very well that, in reality, the opposite was true.

Then they were off to try to enlist the Romans in the conspiracy to murder Jesus.

> **Are you more often concerned with:**
> ❏ **How you appear to others?**
> ❏ **What God sees in your heart?**
> **How do you need to pray about your response?**

NOTES

To the Leader:

Although the daily readings and activities did not cover Peter's denial of Christ, that topic will be addressed in the teaching plan. Carefully read Matthew 26:69-75; Mark 14:66-72; Luke 22:54-62; and John 18:15-18,25-27.

During the Session

1. Request participants name entities that are absolute contrasts (sweet/sour; hope/despair; light/dark). OR Ask: *Have you ever noticed in scary movies that people never turn on the light when they enter a dark room? Do you find yourself urging them to turn on the light? Why?* Agree that we often equate darkness with evil and light with goodness and safety. FOR EITHER OPTION Declare that the contrast between light and dark, between evil and goodness, is very evident in today's lesson. Participants will see the forces of darkness come against the Light of the world.

2. Direct participants to think back on the events they've studied in the first two lessons and state when Jesus' trial before the Sanhedrin must have occurred. Discuss the second activity of Day 1. Ask which translation of John 1:5 participants think best describes the situation. [Both—the darkness didn't comprehend Jesus, but it didn't overcome Him either!] Ask a volunteer to read John 3:19-20. Ask: *Is the Light still in the world? Do people comprehend the Light today? Why?* Discuss the last activity of Day 1. Encourage learners to keep in mind that although that hour of darkness belonged to those who arrested Jesus, the rest of eternity belongs to God.

3. Ask what the Sanhedrin would have had to do to carry out their death penalty against Jesus. [Refer back to the first paragraph of Day 1.] Explain that to obtain some legitimacy with the Roman government the court would have had to make it appear they had reached their verdict during the day, so they reconvened at daybreak. Discuss the first activity of Day 2. Ask: *How did Jesus' reply expose their prejudiced determination to convict Him? What was He implying when He stated He would be seated at God's right hand? What brought the trial to an immediate close?*

4. Invite a volunteer to read Matthew 27:1-5. To discover what happened a short time earlier to another of Jesus' disciples, ask someone to read Matthew 26:69-75. Lead participants to evaluate the

difference between Peter's denial and Judas's betrayal. Explain that Peter displayed cowardice in the heat of the moment. He may have failed Christ at that moment but his faith in Christ, although weak, did not fail. Judas' betrayal, on the other hand, was a deliberate premeditated rejection of Jesus. Use statements and activities from Day 3 to support your explanation.

5. Ask: *What was the difference between Peter's grief and Judas's remorse?* Ask someone to read 2 Corinthians 7:10. Explain that Peter's tears demonstrated immediate repentance. Judas never hated the sin; he just regretted the consequences. Ask: *How might Judas have tried to convince himself that betraying Jesus wasn't that big of a deal? Name ways Christians today try to convince themselves that a sin is no big deal. Who are they fooling?*

6. Request participants state what Judas did to try to escape sin's consequences (Day 4). Ask why Judas was so desperate to get rid of the money. Discuss the second activity of Day 4. Request someone read aloud Matthew 6:23-24. Discuss how Judas sadly discovered the truth of Jesus' words. Discuss the third activity of Day 4. Ask the class to compare the difference between Peter's and Judas's response to their failures. Lead the class to combine Matthew 27:5 with Acts 1:18 to gain a full understanding of Judas's death. Ask someone to read Matthew 8:12. Declare that Judas's failure led to darkness because he gave up on Christ and gave in to despair while Peter's failure led to light because he never gave in to despair and never gave up on Jesus. Invite a volunteer to read aloud Luke 22:31-32. Invite participants to recall ways Peter strengthened believers. Read 1 Peter 2:9-10. Ask: *How do you think Peter's denial of Jesus might have led him to write such encouraging words to believers?* Discuss how believers can use their failures and God's resulting grace to strengthen others.

7. Discuss the first activity of Day 5. Determine how the chief priests' treatment of the money revealed the darkness in which they were living. Explore how hypocrisy leads a person into deeper and deeper darkness. Read John 8:12. Ask: *How can we be protected against this darkness that doomed Judas and the religious leaders?* Read Colossians 1:13-14 and close in prayer, thanking God for rescuing believers from the domain of darkness.

What Will Pilate Do with Jesus?

day One

The Jews First, Then the Romans

Immediately after the early-morning hearing in which the Sanhedrin reaffirmed their death sentence against Jesus, they bound Him and marched Him off to the Roman governor of Judea, Pontius Pilate (Matt. 27:2).

Read John 19:10. What kind of authority did Pilate have over criminal cases?

All criminal penalties in Judea were subject to Pilate's ultimate approval or veto (either directly or through courts that operated under his oversight). The Sanhedrin constituted a religious court, not a civil one. Their jurisdiction covered matters directly pertaining to the Jewish religion. They had no authority to put anyone to death without prior Roman approval (John 18:31)—even in cases where Old Testament law prescribed death. That meant many Old Testament moral and religious standards could not be enforced with biblical penalties. The Romans rarely approved the death penalty in cases of adultery, homosexuality, blasphemy, false prophecy—or other moral or religious transgressions.

That policy was widely resented as a Roman intrusion into the Jewish religion—and an affront to the law of God. It was one of the main points of constant friction between the Sanhedrin and the Roman government. Nonetheless, the members of the Sanhedrin on this occasion were eager to get Roman consent to Jesus' death because that would help legitimize what they were doing. Perhaps they somehow thought if they could dupe the Roman government into killing Jesus, His blood would not be on their hands.

As you read in the margin the list of sins God hates, underline those sins the members of the Sanhedrin were guilty of committing.

The Sanhedrin originally found Pilate unwilling to add his imprimatur to their conspiracy, but in the end Pilate decided it was politically expedient for him to kill Jesus. Pilate's political ambitions thus took precedence over whatever moral convictions he might have had, and he was the one who finally signed the death warrant to murder Jesus.

Have you sought to achieve your own ambitions more like:
❑ **Pilate—with moral compromise or**
❑ **Jesus—with moral conviction?**

Within eighteen hours after His arrest, Jesus was subjected to two trials, each with three phases. In His trial before the Sanhedrin, there had been three hearings—one before Annas, one before the Sanhedrin at night with Caiaphas presiding, and one in the early morning, where the formal verdict was finalized. The Roman trial would also have three phases, as Christ is first brought to Pilate; then sent to Herod; then brought before Pilate once more.

Pilate's Jerusalem residence was known as the Praetorium. It was more than just his residence; it also housed the judgment hall from which he adjudicated all cases brought before him. Its location is disputed, but it was situated either next to Herod's palace or perhaps more likely, adjacent to the Antonia fortress, the nerve center of Roman military power in Jerusalem, directly north of the temple compound. Pilate's *permanent* residence was actually in Caesarea, a town west of Jerusalem on Israel's Mediterranean coast, but he came to Jerusalem during the Jewish feasts, and thus he was in town for the Passover.

"There are six things which the LORD hates, Yes, seven which are an abomination to Him: Haughty eyes, a lying tongue, and hands that shed innocent blood, a heart that devises wicked plans, feet that run rapidly to evil, a false witness who utters lies, and one who spreads strife among brothers" (Prov. 6:16-19 , NASB).

The Sanhedrin's Flip Flop

It was still very early in the morning on Friday—probably before 5:00—when the Sanhedrin arrived at the Praetorium with Jesus in shackles. Pilate could not have known beforehand of their coming, and he probably had to be awakened to meet with them at such an hour.

Read John 18:28-32. Why didn't the Jewish leaders enter Pilate's residence?

_____

"Pilate then went out to them"—probably addressing them from a portico or balcony of the mansion.

A difference in how days were reckoned made it possible for Passover to be celebrated over a two-day period. Galilean Jews reckoned their days from sunrise to sunrise, and so their Passover (14 Nisan) fell on Thursday. That is why Jesus and the disciples had already eaten the Passover meal the preceding evening. But in Judea, where days were counted by the Sadducees' method—from sundown to sundown—14 Nisan was Friday. So the Passover meal would not be eaten by most Judean Jews until later that evening. The Sanhedrin therefore would not enter Pilate's residence because rabbinical tradition (not Scripture) taught that if they entered the home of a Gentile, they would be ceremonially defiled and unable to partake of the Passover feast. Therefore they insisted on meeting Pilate outside.

The melodrama of their refusing to enter the Praetorium actually worked in favor of the Sanhedrin's purpose, which was the political intimidation of Pilate. They had deliberately come en masse (Luke 23:1) and at such an early hour on a feast day in order to lend a sense of the utmost urgency to their plea. Here was a case that clearly could not wait. The early-morning hour, the Sanhedrin's insistence on dealing with this case before they celebrated their feast, and the ploy of bringing Pilate out to meet them on their own ground all worked to underscore in Pilate's mind that this

"Then the whole body of them got up and brought Him before Pilate" (Luke 23:1, NASB).

was an extremely volatile and urgent situation. The Sanhedrin no doubt hoped Pilate would simply do whatever they told him because it was obviously advantageous for him to keep the ruling priests happy during the feast days with so many Jewish pilgrims in town.

But Pilate was unwilling to be made their puppet so easily. He would not approve their sentence against Jesus without first hearing formal charges. So he asked them, "What accusation do you bring against this Man?" (John 18:29).

Their reply was deliberately evasive. They had actually convicted Jesus on charges of blasphemy, but they knew such a charge alone would normally be insufficient to elicit Pilate's approval for an execution. So "they answered and said to him, 'If He were not an evildoer, we would not have delivered Him up to you'" (v. 30).

The arrogance of the reply is astonishing. The Sanhedrin was in effect demanding that Pilate take Jesus and execute Him without asking any questions about what He had been accused of or why He was condemned. They pretended Pilate was impugning their integrity by trying to investigate the charges against Jesus, but the fact is that Pilate's question was one of the few proper legal procedures that was followed in all the hearings Jesus was subjected to. Pilate was refusing to hear Jesus' case until he heard the indictment.

The Sanhedrin's brash reply evidently had the desired effect on Pilate, however, because "Then Pilate said to them, 'You take Him and judge Him according to your law'" (v. 31). In effect, he gave them approval to do with Jesus whatever their law demanded. In all likelihood, Pilate assumed they would eagerly accept his nod of approval and immediately take Jesus out and stone Him. He was in essence telling the Sanhedrin that if they wanted to put Jesus to death for His supposed crimes against Judaism, Rome would turn a blind eye to the deed this time. Pilate obviously had no desire to rile the Sanhedrin on this occasion.

But the Sanhedrin was not satisfied with Pilate's approval to stone Jesus themselves. They wanted a Roman execution. This was their plan for a number of reasons.

Read Matthew 26:5. What did the Sanhedrin and Pilate have in common?
❏ **Utmost respect for the law**
❏ **Fear of the people's opinions**
❏ **Desire for peace**

All along, the Sanhedrin had been eager to avoid responsibility for their actions, and stoning Him by their own hands would ultimately make it impossible for them to do so. Turning Jesus over to the Romans made their plot so much more tidy. Furthermore, according to a tradition similar to the one that forbade them to partake of the feast after entering a Gentile's house, they would have been defiled if they had stoned Jesus before eating the Passover. And now that their plot against Him was moving ahead so quickly, they had apparently decided that they did not want to delay the execution until after Passover (Matt. 26:5). So they were determined to get Pilate to do the deed for them. Once they saw how easily intimidated he was, their determination only intensified.

So they told Pilate, "It is not lawful for us to put anyone to death" (John 18:31). They reminded Pilate of the very restriction they resented so much. In this case, they were determined to use it to their advantage by intimidating Pilate further until he agreed to have Jesus put to death by Roman hands.

All of this, again, perfectly fulfilled the plan of God. By insisting on a Roman execution, the Sanhedrin was unwittingly ensuring "that the saying of Jesus might be fulfilled which He spoke, signifying by what death He would die" (v. 32).

Read Matthew 20:18-19. Jesus had told His disciples He would die by _____ at the hands of

_____.

By handing Jesus over for execution to the Romans, the Sanhedrin brought about the fulfillment of Jesus' own words.

But Pilate insisted on hearing an indictment against Jesus, so if the Sanhedrin wanted Pilate to execute Him, they now needed more substantial charges against Him. They would have to accuse Him of crimes that would stimulate a Roman's appetite for justice more than the accusation of blasphemy would.

Read Luke 23:2. What charges did the Sanhedrin fabricate against Jesus?

_____

_____

In other words, they portrayed Him to Pilate as an insurrectionist who had deliberately stirred the people against Roman taxation and made Himself out to be a king.

None of those things were true, of course—and Pilate clearly knew it (Matt. 27:18). If there had been any real basis for such charges, it would no doubt have come to Pilate's attention first. Furthermore, Pilate knew that the Sanhedrin would not be the ones to try Him for crimes such as those. After all, opposition to Roman taxation was well known and widespread among the Jewish leaders themselves. So the charges against Him were lies. Jesus had never sought to establish a political kingdom in opposition to Rome, but quite the opposite (see John 6:15).

day Three

Pilate's Verdict

At this point, Pilate decided to bring Jesus into the Praetorium and examine Him. Matthew, Mark, and Luke all give a very abbreviated account of the examination: "Jesus stood before the governor. And the governor asked Him, saying, 'Are You the King of the Jews?' So Jesus said to him, 'It is as you say' " (Matt. 27:11).

Read John's fuller account of the exchange that took place in John 18:33–37.

Record the questions Pilate asked Jesus in:

Verse 33 _____

Verse 35b _____

Verse 37 _____

Verse 38 _____

Pilate clearly was aware that the Sanhedrin's charges against Jesus were baseless. But he was in a dilemma. On the one hand, he could not afford to aggravate the Sanhedrin. On the other hand, he did not want to be made their puppet. By bringing Jesus inside and questioning Him directly, he perhaps hoped to get a better assessment of the facts of the case so that he could understand why the Sanhedrin felt Jesus posed such an urgent danger. Jesus' replies probably convinced Pilate that the whole matter was an internal religious dispute. It was clear that Jesus did claim to be a king. But it was also clear that His "kingdom" posed no immediate political threat to Rome.

The whole exchange seems to have only heightened Pilate's exasperation. He was evidently surprised and somewhat taken aback when Jesus answered his first question with a question. Pilate retorted with yet another question, then demanded that Jesus explain what He had done to merit so much animosity from the Sanhedrin. Jesus responded by answering Pilate's first question in a way that must have seemed cryptic to Pilate. He had no capacity for understanding what Jesus meant by a kingdom that is "not of this world"—much less what He meant by "truth."

Compare John 18:38 with John 14:6.
What was the sad irony of Pilate's question?

_____

"What is truth?" was a rhetorical question, merely an expression of Pilate's extreme frustration. It also reveals Pilate's cynical pragmatism about matters of truth. "Truth" to Pilate was defined in utilitarian terms. He stood ready to embrace as "truth" anything that advanced his political agenda. He was not interested in any other kind of truth—especially *spiritual* truth. He hadn't asked the question because he was looking for an answer. After all, the One who was Truth incarnate was standing before him, and if Pilate had been serious about seeking the truth, all he had to do was knock and the door would be opened to him (Matt. 7:7–8). But what Pilate was really concerned about was finding a way out of the political dilemma the Sanhedrin had placed him in.

Pilate's real attitude toward "truth" is seen in the fact that he didn't even wait for a reply. "And when he had said this, he went out again to the Jews, and said to them, 'I find no fault in Him at all' " (John 18:38).

According to Luke 23:5, printed in the margin, what effect did Pilate's declaration of Jesus' innocence have on the Sanhedrin?

_____

"So Pilate said to the chief priests and the crowd, 'I find no fault in this Man.' But they were the more fierce, saying, 'He stirs up the people, teaching throughout all Judea, beginning from Galilee to this place' " (Luke 23:4-5, KJV).

day Four

Jesus' Silence

At this point Jesus was probably being held by Roman soldiers next to Pilate on the balcony of the Praetorium. Matthew writes, "And while He was being accused by the chief priests and elders, He answered nothing. Then Pilate said to Him, 'Do You not hear how many things they testify against You?' But He answered him not one word, so that the governor marveled greatly" (Matt. 27:12–14).

Pilate knew full well that Jesus was innocent of the wrongs they accused Him of.

Read Matthew 27:18. It was obvious to Pilate that the Sanhedrin was motivated by (circle one):

Religious zeal　　　　　**Envy**　　　　　**National fervor**

Pilate had examined Jesus and found no fault in Him. He had already publicly pronounced Him innocent. The case should have been closed, Jesus should have been released, and Pilate should have dispersed the mob. But he was still too fearful of the political implications of offending the Sanhedrin.

Pilate had seen hundreds—perhaps thousands—of accused criminals. *All* of them, innocent and guilty alike, vigorously protested their innocence at every opportunity. Never before had Pilate encountered anyone so manifestly innocent who nonetheless declined to speak in His own defense. Pilate was astonished and bewildered at Jesus' serene and majestic silence. He practically begged Jesus to lash back verbally at His accusers. But Jesus held His silence.

How do you feel about Jesus' silence? (Circle one.)

Frustrated　　　　　**Amazed**　　　　　**Impressed**

Other: _____

49

What could Jesus have said that would have changed the circumstances?

_____

What was there to say? Whom was there to convince? What charges were on the table worth answering? Pilate had already declared Him innocent of any wrongdoing. The Sanhedrin also knew of His innocence and were simply determined to put Him to death anyway. It would have changed nothing for Jesus to speak in His own defense at this point, and so He held His peace.

Once again, this was all a perfect fulfillment of the divine plan. Hundreds of years before, Isaiah wrote of Christ's sacrificial self-offering: "He was oppressed and He was afflicted, yet He opened not His mouth; He was led as a lamb to the slaughter, and as a sheep before its shearers is silent, so He opened not His mouth" (Isa. 53:7).

"O that you would be completely silent, and that it would become your wisdom!"
(Job 13:5 , NASB).

"But he who restrains his lips is wise"
(Prov. 10:19b , NASB).

"Therefore at such a time the prudent person keeps silent, for it is an evil time"
(Amos 5:13 , NASB).

Read the verses in the margin. Indicate on the scale below how well you demonstrate the Lord's wisdom of silence.

Not at all   **Completely**

Let's Play "Hot Potato"

It was obvious to everyone that Pilate was in a serious political predicament with Christ on trial before him. He had no legitimate grounds on which to execute Jesus, and yet he could not afford to anger the Jewish leaders over an issue they quite clearly regarded as urgent. For their part, the Sanhedrin were determined to press their charges against Jesus, knowing the leverage they had with Pilate, who didn't need any more bad press going back to Rome.

Suddenly an idea occurred to Pilate that might help him extricate himself from this dilemma. It was prompted by something someone said in one of the many accusations that were made against Jesus.

Read Luke 23:5-7.
What detail in the Sanhedrin's accusation did Pilate latch on to?

_____

What loophole out of his predicament did Pilate think he'd found?

_____

Galilee lay outside Pilate's area of jurisdiction. It belonged to the region ruled by Herod Antipas. Pilate realized that if Jesus were a Galilean, he might be able to hand the whole controversy off to Herod, who was also in town for Passover season.

Read what Luke said of Pilate at this point in Luke 23:6–8.

So Pilate had Jesus marched over to Herod's palace—a fairly short walk through the narrow city streets. By now more of the city would be awakening. The movement of the military escort, the Sanhedrin, and the accumulating crowd would have drawn still more people to see what was happening. Word began to spread through Jerusalem. Jesus was on trial. Throngs of curiosity seekers came to see for themselves.

This week's title asks, "What Will Pilate Do with Jesus?" The more important question is, "What will you do with Jesus?"
❑ **Seek to do away with Him like the Sanhedrin**
❑ **Attempt to evade your responsibility to Him like Pilate**
❑ **Come see Him out of curiosity like the crowds**
❑ **Commit your life to Him in full surrender**

To the Leader:

Pray that God will use this lesson to cause participants to consider what they have done with Jesus. Depending on the persons in your class and especially the Holy Spirit's direction, you may want to conclude this week's lesson by giving people the opportunity to respond to Christ in full surrender of their lives. Be prepared to share the plan of salvation (see the inside cover of this publication) in a personal, compelling manner.

During the Session

1. Ask why participants think John F. Kennedy said, "Mothers all want their sons to grow up to be president, but they don't want them to become politicians in the process."[1] Ask: *What negative impressions about politicians do people often have?* State that the negative side of politics is very evident in Pilate's treatment of Jesus. OR Invite participants to identify people they would trust completely to care for their children. Ask them to state why they would do this. Then ask them to state the type of people they absolutely would not want to be near their children. Declare that historians describe Pilate as a harsh, ruthless governor with a strong contempt for Jews. The fact God would allow His Son to be in this man's hands is another indication of the amazing sacrifice He made on behalf of humanity.

2. Invite someone to read John 18:28. Ask participants to state from Day 1 why the Sanhedrin took Jesus to Pilate and how that was evidence of their hypocrisy. Ask the first question of Day 2. Discuss the irony of the Sanhedrin's refusal to enter Pilate's house. (You may choose to use the second activity of Day 1 to point out that the Sanhedrin had broken many of God's laws but refused to break tradition.) Request participants describe how the Sanhedrin sought to intimidate Pilate and what they hoped to accomplish through their manipulative tactics. [See Day 2.] Ask: *How do you think the Sanhedrin knew they could manipulate Pilate so easily? How can others know we are people who can't be manipulated or intimidated?*

3. Ask a volunteer to read aloud John 18:29-31. Lead a discussion with questions such as: *How did Pilate show some backbone at first? What was the Sanhedrin implying in verse 30? What was Pilate actually giving them the approval to do by his answer? Why wasn't the Sanhedrin satisfied with this solution? What political games were Pilate and the Sanhedrin playing?* Discuss the second activity of Day 2. Ask: *Why would it make things easier for the Jewish leaders if Jesus was killed by the Romans? How was the Sanhedrin's plot actually fulfilling Jesus' words in Matthew 20:18-19?* [See the third activity of Day 2.]

4. Invite someone to read Luke 23:1-2. Inquire: *Why didn't the Sanhedrin stick with their original charge of blasphemy against Jesus? Which of the charges were true?* Read John 6:15 and state that Jesus turned aside opportunities to be made king, so that charge was false. Invite someone to read Mark 12:13-17. Ask what Jesus really taught about paying taxes to Caesar.

5. Note that Pilate began to examine the accusation that Jesus claimed to be a King. Discuss the first activity of Day 3. Ask: *What do you think Jesus meant by His question in John 18:34—was He trying to confuse Pilate or was He trying to help Pilate examine himself?* Declare that Jesus wants each person to personally seek Him and not just go on what they've heard others say about Him. Discuss the second activity of Day 3. Ask why people today fail to see the truth that is right in front of them (you may want to refer to Rom. 1:18-21). Ask what Pilate's conclusion was after examining Jesus and how the Sanhedrin responded to his verdict (last activity of Day 3).

6. Discuss the first activity of Day 4. Direct participants to read John 11:47-48 and 12:9-11 and state why they were envious of Jesus. Ask: *If Pilate knew all the charges were jealously made up and he knew Jesus was innocent, why didn't he release Jesus immediately?* Invite someone to read Matthew 27:12-14. Ask: *What do you think Pilate wanted Jesus to say?* Discuss the second activity of Day 4.

7. Discuss the first activity of Day 5. Ask: *How have you observed Pilate playing politics throughout this entire lesson?* Request participants prayerfully consider the final activity in Day 1. Ask: *What was the Sanhedrin trying to protect by killing Jesus? What was Pilate trying to protect by yielding to them?* Declare they all ended up condemning themselves because people cannot play politics with God. He will call all persons to account for what each has done with His Son. Lead the class to explore how people respond to Jesus in the four ways listed in the final activity of Day 5. Urge participants to respond to Jesus in full surrender.

[1] Quote DB: Politics [on line], 2005 [cited 6 Sept. 2006]. Available from the Internet: *http://www.quotedb.com/categories/politics*.

The Roman Trials Continue

day One

Herod's Turn

No one was more curious or more eager to lay eyes on Jesus than Herod.

Read Luke 23:6-12. Why was Herod eager to see Jesus?

_____

Herod Antipas was the same member of the Herodian dynasty who had killed John the Baptist a couple of years before (Matt. 14:1–12). His main palace was located in the city of Tiberias, a spectacular, sparkling, new town on the west shore of the Sea of Galilee, only ten miles or so from Capernaum (Peter's hometown and Jesus' base of operations). Herod himself had built Tiberias less than ten years before. He had named it in honor of Caesar.

Jesus' ministry covered the entire Galilee region, but there is no mention in Scripture that He ever visited Tiberias. It may be that Jesus was deliberately keeping His distance from Herod. There were rumors that Herod was also seeking to kill Jesus. Therefore, even though Herod and Jesus had lived quite literally within walking distance of each other for several years, and Herod was well familiar with Jesus' reputation, this was Herod's first opportunity to see Jesus with his own eyes.

Read Luke 22:63 and Matthew 26:67. Do you think Herod saw what he expected when Jesus appeared before him? ❏ Yes ❏ No

Why? _____

How different Christ must have looked from the strong, prophetic miracle worker Herod expected to see! His face was already badly bruised and swollen from the abuse He had taken. Spittle and blood were drying in His matted hair. Tired and physically weakened from a sleepless night, He stood before Herod, bound and under guard like a common criminal.

Most disappointing to Herod was Jesus' refusal to perform for him. Herod "questioned Him with many words, but He answered him nothing" (Luke 23:9). The Sanhedrin was still dogging Christ, standing nearby and vehemently shouting denunciation and accusations at Him (v. 10). But Jesus refused to utter even so much as a word. In *all* the various hearings and examinations He was subjected to, He was astonishingly quiet (Matt. 27:14)—always refusing to rail at His accusers or say anything in self-defense (1 Pet. 2:23). But only before Herod did He remain in utter and complete silence. In the first place, Herod had no legitimate jurisdiction in Jerusalem. If Herod intended to impose any sentence in this case, Jesus would first have to be taken back to Galilee and put on trial there. So Jesus had no legal obligation to answer him anyway. But there may have been another reason Jesus kept silent. Herod's treatment of Jesus' forerunner, John the Baptist, made clear where he stood regarding the truth of Christ. Silence was the only appropriate response under such circumstances.

After a short time, Herod grew tired of questioning Jesus and decided to make sport of Him. "Then Herod, with his men of war, treated Him with contempt and mocked Him, arrayed Him in a gorgeous robe, and sent Him back to Pilate" (Luke 23:11). Luke adds a historical footnote: "That very day Pilate and Herod became friends with each other, for previously they had been at enmity with each other" (v. 12). It was an unholy alliance—a friendship based on the one thing they had in common: their cowardly and contemptuous treatment of Christ.

Both Herod and Pilate knew that Christ posed no immediate threat to their political interests. His appearance and His demeanor spoke for themselves. How could such a passive, serene, fragile person—whose claim to fame was as a teacher and a healer—pose any political threat to anyone? It was as clear to Herod as it had been to Pilate that the Sanhedrin's charges were fabricated and ill-motivated. But Herod happily joined in the game. He clothed Jesus in a gorgeous robe. Then Herod and his security forces subjected Jesus to mockery and contempt before the growing crowd of

onlookers. Finally, after satisfying his desire for amusement at the expense of Jesus, Herod sent Him back to Pilate.

How do you usually respond when Jesus doesn't do what you want Him to do for you?
❑ **I mock His ability and desire to care for me.**
❑ **I get angry and feel sorry for myself.**
❑ **I trust Him to do what's best for me.**
❑ **Other:**

_____

day Two

A Proposed Prisoner Swap

Jesus' own refusal to speak to Herod helped force the trial back into Pilate's court. Pilate must have been surprised and somewhat frustrated when the Sanhedrin returned with Jesus and a larger-than-ever crowd of onlookers in tow. Things were only getting further out of hand, and now it would be harder than ever for Pilate to end the matter without creating a scandal Rome would hear about or a riot in Jerusalem at the time of the busiest Jewish festival. Pilate therefore decided to try to act the statesman and bring an end to the matter with a compromise of sorts.

Read what Luke says Pilate decided in Luke 23:13–16. What compromise did Pilate propose?

_____

Pilate actually proposed Jesus' release in fulfillment of a custom that was in place at the time. As a diplomatic gesture toward the Jews, and in order to promote goodwill on the feast day, the Roman governor would release one Jewish prisoner from Roman custody every Passover. Matthew says, "Now at the feast the governor was accustomed to releasing to the multitude one prisoner whom they wished" (Matt. 27:15). Matthew is not suggesting that the Roman governor would automatically release *whomever* the people wished, allowing them to choose from all the prisoners in custody at the time. Instead, what he means is that a few offenders were selected by Roman officials and those names were given to the people as candidates from which to choose. Rome would grant an automatic pardon to the prisoner the people selected from the names proposed to them.

Pilate seems to have decided to use the custom for his own benefit in a last-ditch effort to escape the dilemma the Sanhedrin had created for him—a conflict between conscience and career; a choice between satisfying the Jews he hated or the Caesar he feared. He gave the people a choice of only *two* prisoners to be released. One was Jesus, whose popularity among the common people was well known. The only other candidate for release Pilate gave them was Barabbas.

According to Matthew 27:16 and Luke 23:18-19,

Barabbas was a _____ criminal who was

imprisoned for _____ and _____.

Barabbas was a miscreant so foul and notorious that Pilate seemed sure the people would never choose him. His crimes had made him infamous, and he was probably both hated and feared by the people. Pilate probably thought his clever ploy would leave the people with no option but to choose Jesus' release over that of Barabbas. That way Pilate could avoid complicity in the Sanhedrin's plot against Jesus. ("For he knew that they had handed Him over because of envy"—Matt. 27:18.) This way Pilate could release Jesus, but rather than being seen as refusing to carry out the will of the Sanhedrin, he would be seen as obeying the will of the people. It was a brilliant diplomatic maneuver.

But it did not work.

Pilate's Wife's Dream

First of all, just as Pilate was preparing to render his final verdict, the scene was interrupted in a most unusual way.

Read Matthew 27:15-19. Who interrupted Pilate and why?

_____

Apparently the message was delivered publicly, so that all present could hear. Thus it served as a warning not only to Pilate but also to the Sanhedrin and the people. God in His merciful providence orchestrated both the dream and the timing of Mrs. Pilate's warning so that all concerned would have one final, gracious alarm-beacon before they proceeded with the monstrously evil deed they planned to carry out.

Note how each of the men below responded to a warning. Then check how you usually respond to warnings.

❑ **Lot's sons-in-law (Gen. 19:14)** _____

❑ **Joseph (Matt. 2:13-14)** _____

❑ **Pilate (Matt. 27:19,26)** _____

As far as Pilate was concerned, his wife's warning only heightened his dilemma. The pressure on him from both sides was increasing, and he was more eager than ever to lay the whole issue to rest.

But the moment court was interrupted by Pilate's wife's message, the Sanhedrin seized the opportunity to rally the people around their cause. They began to spread the word to the crowd that they should choose Barabbas. "The chief priests and elders persuaded the multitudes that they should ask for Barabbas and destroy Jesus" (v. 20). The Sanhedrin was comprised of the spiritual leaders of the land. For them to manipulate the people like this was a gross abuse of their God-given authority. But they found the crowd perfectly willing to be led astray.

Pilate posed the question one more time: "The governor answered and said to them, 'Which of the two do you want me to release to you?' They said, 'Barabbas!' " (v. 21). The answer came back clearly and unanimously, without hesitation.

Pilate was dumbfounded. He asked them, "What then shall I do with Jesus who is called Christ?"

According to Matthew 27:22, the crowd responded,

_____

Pilate, still unable to believe that the entire mob would have such strong feelings against One who had so lately been so popular, asked, " 'Why, what evil has He done?' But they cried out all the more, saying, 'Let Him be crucified!' " (v. 23).

"Wishing to satisfy the crowd, Pilate released Barabbas for them, and after having Jesus scourged, he handed Him over to be crucified" (Mark 15:15 , NASB).

day *Four*

The Governor's Acquiescence

Pilate had reached the end of his rope. He had no desire to participate in the conspiracy against Jesus, but the Jewish leaders had left him little choice. The crowd was now on the verge of a riot. He was finally out of options. Matthew writes, "When Pilate saw that he could not prevail at all, but rather that a tumult was rising, he took water and washed his hands before the multitude, saying, 'I am innocent of the blood of this just Person. You see to it' " (Matt. 27:24).

Read Psalm 24:3-5. Do you think Pilate's clean hands made him innocent? ❏ Yes   ❏ No   ❏ Not sure

Why? _____

The meaning of the ceremonial hand washing would have been poignantly familiar to the crowd. Pilate was expressing contempt for the fact that they had railroaded him into becoming a part of the conspiracy against Jesus. He was giving them what they wanted, but he wanted to make it clear that he was not doing it willingly.

Of course, no ritual hand washing could truly absolve Pilate of the guilt he bore for his part in the crucifixion. He had the power and the responsibility to stop it, but he did not. He was as guilty as the rest, and the fact that he participated out of political expediency rather than overt hatred for Jesus did not nullify or minimize his guilt in the least.

"For truly in this city there were gathered together against Your holy servant Jesus, whom You anointed, both Herod and Pontius Pilate, along with the Gentiles and the peoples of Israel, to do whatever Your hand and Your purpose predestined to occur" (Acts 4:27-28 , NASB).

For their part, the people would have been perfectly happy to absolve Pilate. "All the people answered and said, 'His blood be on us and on our children' " (v. 25). In an amazing act of self-condemnation, they said they would accept the full blame on themselves and their posterity, if that was what it took to get Pilate to let them kill Jesus.

Of course their *saying* that Pilate was absolved from the guilt did not make it so. Scripture makes it perfectly clear that Pilate, Herod, the people of Jerusalem, and the Gentiles who participated in the crucifixion all bore the guilt together (Acts 4:27). But it is an interesting fact of history that just a few short months after this, the same Jewish leaders who had provoked the people to say, "His blood be on us and on our children," were resentful of the disciples' gospel preaching, saying, "You have filled Jerusalem with your doctrine, and intend to bring this Man's blood on us!" (Acts 5:28).

Read Isaiah 1:15. The Jewish leaders knew if they had blood on their hands that God would not

_____ **or** _____.

Pilate had originally hoped to have Jesus flogged and released. According to John's Gospel, Pilate was still seeking a way to release Him, and that may be why he had Him publicly scourged at this point. Perhaps he thought the sight of a Roman scourging would satisfy the crowd's bloodlust.

Scourging alone was sometimes fatal. A Roman scourge was a short wooden handle with numerous long lashes of leather attached to it. Each leather strip had a sharp piece of glass, metal, bone, or other hard object attached to the end of it. The victim would be stripped of all clothing and tied to a post by his wrists with his hands high enough over his head to virtually lift him off the ground. The feet would be dangling, and the skin on the back and buttocks completely taut. One or two scourge-bearers (lictors) would then deliver blows, skillfully laying the lashes diagonally across the back and buttocks with extreme force. The skin would literally be torn away, and often muscles were deeply lacerated. It was not uncommon for the scourge-wounds to penetrate deep into the kidneys or lacerate arteries, causing wounds that in themselves proved fatal. Some victims died from extreme shock during the flogging.

Read John 19:1-4. What did the soldiers do to Jesus after they flogged Him?

_____

The Apostle John records how after Jesus' scourging and the mockery that accompanied it, Pilate once more vainly tried to seek Jesus' release. Pilate brought Jesus again before the crowd, dressed in a robe fashioned from a soldier's tunic, crowned with a crown of thorns, and triumphantly presented Him to the people, probably hoping they would be satisfied that Jesus had suffered enough: "And Pilate said to them, 'Behold the Man!' " (John 19:5). But they were not satisfied. "Therefore, when the chief priests and officers saw Him, they cried out, saying, 'Crucify Him, crucify Him!' " (v. 6).

Pilate, still astonished at the crowd's insatiable thirst for Jesus' blood, said to them, "You take Him and crucify Him, for I find no fault in Him" (v. 6). Still vainly trying to wash his hands of the matter, he repeated his earlier verdict, declaring Jesus' innocence once more.

day *Five*

"Where Are You From?"

The crowd would have none of it. "The Jews answered him, 'We have a law, and according to our law He ought to die, because He made Himself the Son of God.' Therefore, when Pilate heard that saying, he was the more afraid, and went again into the Praetorium, and said to Jesus, 'Where are

You from?' " (vv. 7–9). They were demanding that Pilate follow through with a crucifixion at the hands of Roman authorities. Their mention of His claim to be the Son of God seems to have severely rattled Pilate. His question to Jesus ("Where are you from?") was obviously spoken with a mixture of wonder, amazement, and fear.

"But Jesus gave him no answer" (v. 9).

"Then Pilate said to Him, 'Are You not speaking to me? Do You not know that I have power to crucify You, and power to release You?' Jesus answered, 'You could have no power at all against Me unless it had been given you from above. Therefore the one who delivered Me to you has the greater sin' " (vv. 10–11).

Pilate was by now beginning to see the enormity of his wrong-doing from Jesus' perspective. Perhaps it was merely a superstitious fear on Pilate's part, but he was clearly shaken by Jesus' claim of deity (for Pilate would have correctly understood the implications of the expression "Son of God"). And he wanted no part of the guilt he knew he would bear if such a claim were true, because he had already wrongfully abused Jesus merely by having Him flogged. And even though Pilate was not a believer in the Hebrew God, his Roman polytheistic worldview was laden with superstition about offending the gods and the heavy price one could pay for such an offense.

Furthermore, it must have sent a cold shiver down Pilate's spine when Jesus told him, with quiet composure and a calm, unflappable authority, "You could have no power at all against Me unless it had been given you from above." That seems to be why "From then on Pilate sought to release Him" (v. 12).

"But the Jews cried out, saying, 'If you let this Man go, you are not Caesar's friend. Whoever makes himself a king speaks against Caesar'" (v. 12). This was their trump card against Pilate. This is why they had so much leverage against him: They knew he was concerned about what Caesar would think, and he was especially afraid of what all this could ultimately mean for his career. But the crowd's threat against Pilate was full of irony, since not one of *them* wanted to be thought of as "Caesar's friend." Still, it was an effective, though not very subtle, threat.

"When Pilate therefore heard that saying, he brought Jesus out and sat down in the judgment seat in a place that is called The Pavement, but in Hebrew, Gabbatha" (John 19:13). The Pavement was a stone-paved area adjacent to the Antonio Fortress, where military court was sometimes held and prisoners were detained. The paving stones are there to this day, and some of them still bear marks where Roman soldiers played games while guarding prisoners during hearings. Since the Jewish leaders would not enter Pilate's judgment hall in the Praetorium, Pilate had Jesus taken to Gabbatha for His final judgment. There was a judgment seat there where Pilate could render his final official orders.

Read John's account in John 19:14–16.

Recall from Matthew 26:65-66 the reason the Sanhedrin declared Jesus deserved death.

_____

According to this passage in John 19, how did the chief priests commit blasphemy?

_____

The sixth hour, by Roman calculation, would be 6 a.m., so it was still an extremely early hour. The crowd persisted in their cries for Jesus' crucifixion. Pilate had finally been forced into precisely the circumstances he so desperately wanted to avoid. But he now felt he had no choice, and so he gave the order for Jesus to be crucified. He bartered away his eternal soul for temporary job security.

Rome was thus in full complicity with the Sanhedrin's murderous scheme. Pilate, the highest ruler in the region, had been utterly unable to derail the crucifixion. There was no stopping it now.

How do you most often respond when you are in a situation where Christ is on trial?
❑ **I make a quick escape like the disciples.**
❑ **I join the crowd with little thought of what I'm doing.**
❑ **Like Pilate, I refuse to take a stand.**
❑ **I stand with Jesus regardless of the consequences.**

To the Leader:

As you guide participants to explore how to stand with Christ and choose Him over all other options, be willing to share instances and struggles from your own life. Adults will learn far more from what you *do* than what you *say*.

During the Session

1. Ask: *What do you have to do to keep your job? Where do you draw the line? What will you NOT do to save your job?* State that Pilate's treatment of Jesus' case is a sobering warning to Christian adults to put Jesus ahead of everything, including their careers. OR Challenge participants to identify all individuals involved in a courtroom trial and signify whether that character is neutral, for, or against the defendant. Ask who all was involved in Jesus' trial and whether they were neutral, for, or against Him. State that today's lesson challenges believers to determine to stand with Jesus.

2. Discuss the first two activities of Day 1. Ask: *How did Jesus demonstrate He was in control even while He was under guard? What might a less-than-perfect person have done at this point? How can we remain resolutely committed to Christ even when we're on trial?* Ask a volunteer to read aloud Luke 22:41-42. Point out that Jesus had committed to God's will, including the suffering, before He was ever arrested. Believers must be devoted to prayer and fully committed to God's will before a crisis erupts.

3. Ask: *How do you think Pilate felt when Jesus and an even larger crowd ended up back at his palace?* Discuss the first activity of Day 2. Ask whom Pilate thought he could please with his compromise and whom he actually did please. Ask: *When is compromise good? When is compromise not good?* Lead the class to discuss how believers are tempted to choose compromise over conviction. Ask: *How can we make the right choice?*

4. Instruct participants to read Matthew 27:15-17 and state the choice Pilate gave the crowd. Discuss why Barabbas and Jesus were Pilate's only two options for release. Discuss the first question of Day 3. Lead a discussion with questions such as: *Why do you think Matthew included this episode in his Gospel? Who really was warning Pilate and why? How do you know when you're being warned by God? How do you usually respond?* Invite someone to read aloud Matthew 27:20-23. Ask who else God intended to warn with Mrs. Pilate's message and

how that warning was received. State that Pilate had given the people an option but he was the one who ended up having to make a choice. Request a volunteer read aloud Mark 15:15 from the margin of Day 3. Ask what option Pilate chose and why. Invite volunteers to answer: *How is Barabbas's story your story?*

5. Request someone read aloud Matthew 27:24. Ask: *What products have you found to be the best stain removers? What stains just won't come out? Was washing his hands enough to remove the stain of Pilate's guilt? Why or why not?* Discuss the first activity of Day 4. Ask: *How can we have clean hands* and *a pure heart?* Read Ezekiel 36:26. State that the only way to remove sin's stain is to choose Christ over all other options and let Him purify your heart.

6. Invite someone to read aloud John 19:1-6. Ask why Pilate, after agreeing to have Jesus crucified, still had Him beaten and presented to the crowd wearing a robe and crown. Ask what effect the sight of Jesus' blood had on the crowd. Ask a volunteer to read aloud John 19:7-16. Ask: *Logically, who should have been afraid and who should have been in control at this point? Why? Who actually was afraid? Who was actually in control? Why?* Ask what trump card the crowd used against Pilate and why it was so effective. Discuss why the chief priests' declaration of allegiance to Caesar was so hypocritical.

7. State that Dr. MacArthur said Pilate faced a conflict between his conscience and his career. Lead the class to explore how adults face that same conflict today. Read Dr. MacArthur's statement that Pilate "bartered away his eternal soul for temporary job security." Ask: *How can we make a better—and safer—choice than Pilate did?* Ask two volunteers to read aloud Galatians 1:10 and 1 Thessalonians 2:4. State that unlike Pilate, believers must seek to please God rather than other people.

8. Remark that the last four lessons have focused on Jesus' trials before the Jews and the Romans. Ask: *How is Jesus still put on trial today? How can we be people who stand with Jesus regardless of the consequences?* Discuss their responses.

9. Close in prayer.

Murder at Golgotha

day One

The Mockery

The flogging administered by Pilate was merely the beginning of a long series of physical and emotional tortures that would finally culminate in the death of Jesus. It was accompanied by cruel mockery, which the pagan Roman soldiers apparently administered purely for their own amusement.

Read Matthew's description of the scene in Matthew 27:26–30. In the margin, list all the ways the soldiers mocked Jesus.

Despite the fact that these soldiers had no reason whatsoever to heap such scorn on Jesus, they evidently took great delight in doing so. These were men hardened by having witnessed numerous executions, so the pain of such torture no longer made any impact whatsoever on them. As far as they were concerned, Jesus was merely another religious fanatic with whom they were free to amuse themselves as cruelly as they pleased.

Pilate's orders were to scourge and crucify Jesus, but the cruel mockery they heaped on Him reveals their own wickedness. As they led Jesus back to the Praetorium, they deliberately made a spectacle of Him for the amusement of the taunting crowd. The tumult drew the entire garrison of soldiers to watch.

A Roman cohort consisted of six hundred soldiers. These soldiers were stationed at the Antonio Fortress (which overlooked the temple mount from the north). They were an elite unit, assigned to serve the governor and to keep the peace that was so fragile in this most volatile region of the Roman Empire. Rome conscripted soldiers from all the regions it conquered, but Jews were exempt from military service, so all these soldiers would have been Gentiles. They were probably Syrian troops because Syrians spoke

Aramaic, and this would have been essential in Jerusalem. They probably had little knowledge of who He was. As far as they were concerned, He was just one in a long line of religious zealots who had troubled the peace and made problems for Rome. They undoubtedly assumed that He deserved whatever ridicule and torment they could heap on Him. Condemned Roman prisoners were considered fair game for such abuse, as long as they were not killed before the sentence of crucifixion could be carried out. The soldiers' abuse of Jesus was probably not motivated by any personal animosity toward Him, but rarely did they have such enthusiastic crowds to play to. They evidently decided to make the most of it.

Jesus had already been slapped and beaten repeatedly, even before He was delivered to Pilate, so His face was undoubtedly swollen and bleeding already. After the scourging, His back would be a mass of bleeding wounds and quivering muscles, and the robe they fashioned for Him would only add to the pain of those wounds. They stripped Him of His own garments, which suggests He was quite literally naked apart from the robe they fashioned for Him. The robe was apparently made from an old tunic— probably an old garment that had been discarded by one of the soldiers. (The Greek expression is *chlamus,* signifying a military cloak; not the same "gorgeous robe"—*esthes*—used by Herod in Luke 23:11). Matthew says the robe was scarlet, but Mark and John call it "purple" (Mark 15:17; John 19:2)—suggesting that it was a badly faded tunic. It was probably the nearest thing to purple (signifying royalty) the soldiers could find.

Their aim was clearly to make a complete mockery of Jesus' claim that He was a king. To that end, they fashioned a crown of thorns. Caesar wore a laurel wreath as a crown; thorns were a cruel corruption of that. These were no doubt the longest, sharpest thorns that could be found; many varieties of these grow in Jerusalem to this day—some with two-inch barbed quills that would penetrate deep into His head as the crown was pressed hard upon Him.

The reed in Jesus' hand was a further attempt to lampoon His royal claim. The reed represented a scepter—but was a weak, frail imitation of the scepter Caesar carried on festive state occasions.

Read Isaiah 62:3-4. Why did Jesus endure the mockery of the fake crown and scepter?

They showed their utter contempt for Him by feigning the sort of veneration one would show to royalty, bowing at His feet, but saying "Hail, King of the Jews!" in jeering tones. Then, as the Jewish priests had done, they spat on Him, and one of them took the reed and used it to strike Jesus repeatedly on His head. The reed, though a flimsy scepter, would have been firm enough to inflict great pain on His already battered head. The Apostle John records that they also struck Him with their hands (John 19:3)—probably slapping with open hands while taunting Him some more.

According to Matthew 27:31, after the soldiers

mocked Jesus, they _____.

day Two

The Shame

Victims of crucifixion were usually made to wear a placard around their neck on which was written the crime they were condemned for. It was part of the shame that was deliberately inflicted on victims of crucifixion. They were led through the streets and made to walk in a public procession in order to maximize the humiliation of the spectacle.

Read Hebrews 12:2. Jesus was able to bear the shame because:
❏ **He was too exhausted to care.**
❏ **He was so angry at the injustice being committed.**
❏ **He was focused on the joy that awaited Him.**

Such victims were also forced to carry their own cross to the place of execution. Some have suggested that Roman victims were made to carry only the lateral crossbeam (known as the *patibulum),* which was later attached to the top of a vertical beam that was already planted firmly in the ground. But Scripture seems to indicate that Christ was bearing the entire cross. A Roman cross large enough to crucify a grown man might weigh as much as two hundred pounds—an extremely heavy load to bear in any circumstances. But for someone in Jesus' already weakened condition it would be virtually impossible to drag such a load from the Praetorium to a place of crucifixion outside the walls of Jerusalem.

Matthew records that Jesus needed help bearing His cross: "Now as they came out, they found a man of Cyrene, Simon by name. Him they compelled to bear His cross" (27:32). At least four soldiers— a quaternion—would accompany the victim to the execution site. The soldiers evidently grew impatient with Jesus' agonizing pace, and they grabbed Simon along the way, conscripting him to carry the cross for Jesus.

Even with Simon carrying His cross, Jesus apparently was too weak to walk unsupported. Mark 15:22 says, "they brought Him to the place Golgotha," using a Greek expression for "brought" that suggests He was actually borne along to that place—probably walking with much difficulty, needing constant support from the soldiers along the way.

Read Mark 15:21. What else do you learn about this man Simon?

Simon the Cyrene was no idle spectator wishing to mock Jesus like the rest of the crowd. Cyrene was an African city on the Mediterranean coast—in what is Libya today. A large Jewish community lived there, and Simon was probably a Jewish pilgrim who had made the long journey from Cyrene to Jerusalem for the Passover. Mark probably was writing from Rome around A.D. 50, so Alexander and Rufus were probably believers known to the church there. The fact that Simon is named in all three Synoptic Gospels suggests that his later history was known to the gospel writers, and that undoubtedly means he later became a believer in Christ. Though he could not have been pleased about being conscripted to carry a condemned criminal's cross, it became a doorway to eternal life for him.

Read Luke 23:26-31. Simon heard Christ's last public message on the road to Calvary. What do you think impressed him about this man he was forced to serve?

Part of the message was a reference to Hosea 10:8. It was a dire warning of disaster to come. Since in that culture childbearing was understood to be the highest blessing God could give a woman, only the worst kind of plague or disaster could ever cause anyone to say "Blessed are the barren, wombs that never bore, and breasts which never nursed!" The green tree represented a time of abundance and blessing, and the dry tree stood for bad times. Jesus was saying that if a tragedy like this could happen in good times, what would befall the nation in bad times? If the Romans crucified someone whom they admitted was guilty of no offense, what would they do to the Jewish nation when they rebelled? Christ was referring to events that would happen less than a generation later, in A.D. 70, when the Roman army would lay siege to Jerusalem, utterly destroy the temple, and slaughter thousands upon thousands of Jewish people—multitudes of them by crucifixion. Christ had spoken of the coming holocaust before (see Luke 19:41–44). His awareness of that approaching catastrophe still weighed heavily on His mind as He made His way to the cross.

day Three

The Curse

Crucifixion was a particularly execrable way to die. In the Jewish mind it was tantamount to the hanging on a tree Moses described in Deuteronomy 21:22–23.

Read Deuteronomy 21:22-23, printed in the margin, and underline the ultimate fate of the one crucified.

The Mosaic law also required that all executions occur outside the city walls (Num. 15:35; see Heb. 13:12).

The Romans had a slightly different concept. They made sure that all crucifixions took place near major thoroughfares in order to make the condemned person a public example for all passersby. So Jesus' crucifixion took place outside the city, but in a heavily trafficked location carefully selected to make Him a public spectacle.

The place where Jesus was crucified was called Calvary (a Latin adaptation of the Greek term that appears in the biblical text: *kranion,* "a skull"—Luke 23:33). The Aramaic name for it was Golgotha, also meaning "a skull." Nowhere in Scripture is it called a hill, but it is generally assumed that this spoke of a promontory, craggy knoll, or incline that had the appearance of a skull.

Read Matthew 27:33-34. The soldiers gave Jesus

_____ but Jesus _____.

Apparently just before they nailed Jesus to the cross, the soldiers offered Him this bitter drink. "Sour wine" is vinegar. "Gall" is something that tastes bitter. Mark 15:23 says the bitter substance was myrrh, which acts as a mild narcotic. The soldiers may have offered it for its numbing effect just before they drove the nails through the flesh. When Jesus tasted what it was, He spat it out. He did not want His senses numbed.

Read Matthew 26:39.

Whose cup was Jesus committed to drink?_____

What was in that cup? _____

Jesus had come to the cross to be a sin bearer, and He would feel the full effect of the sin He bore; He would endure the full measure of its pain. He would not anesthetize His senses before He had accomplished all His work. In fact, the vinegar and gall fulfilled a messianic prophecy from Psalm 69:19–21.

Read Psalm 69:19-21 and complete the following:

When Jesus needed comfort, He was given

_____.

When Jesus needed something to drink, He was given

_____.

The Pain

"Then they crucified Him" (Matt. 27:35). Crucifixion was a form of execution that the Romans had learned from the Persians. It was also practiced in pre-Roman times in Phoenicia, Carthage, and Egypt. But it evidently originated in Persia. The Persians believed that earth, fire, and water were sacred elements, and all customary methods of execution defiled the sacred elements. So the Persians developed a method of crucifying victims by impaling them on a pole, thus raising them high above the earth, where they were left to die. Later cultures developed different methods of crucifixion, and Rome employed several of them.

What do we learn about Jesus' crucifixion from Thomas's remarks in John 20:25?

_____

By the time of Christ, crucifixion had become the favored method of execution throughout the Roman Empire, and especially in Judea, where it was regularly used to make a public example of rioters and insurrectionists. According to Josephus, after Herod the Great died, the Roman governor of Syria, Quinctilius Varus, crucified two thousand men in order to quell an uprising. Josephus also says that Titus crucified so many people when he sacked Jerusalem in A.D. 70 that there was no wood left for crosses and no place left to set them up. By the time of Christ, Rome had already crucified more than thirty thousand victims in and around Judea. So crosses with dead or dying men hanging on them were a common sight around Jerusalem, and a constant reminder of Roman brutality.

Read Psalm 22:14-17. Use this messianic prophecy to describe some of the pain Jesus endured.

_____

The Humiliation

Aside from the physical pain of crucifixion, the most notable feature of this type of execution was the stigma of disgrace that was attached to it. Victims were mercilessly taunted. They were usually hanged naked. They were deliberately made a spectacle of shame and reproach.

Scripture indicates that Christ was deliberately stripped of all clothing and dignity when He was crucified. In fact, the soldiers who kept guard over Him gambled for what remained of His clothing. Matthew writes, "Then they crucified Him, and divided His garments, casting lots, that it might be fulfilled which was spoken by the prophet: 'They divided My garments among them, and for My clothing they cast lots.' Sitting down, they kept watch over Him there" (Matt. 27:35–36). The prophecy referred to is Psalm 22:18, which foretold the casting of lots for Jesus' clothes.

> "They divide my garments among them, and for my clothing they cast lots" (Ps. 22:18 , NASB).

There may have been as many as five pieces of clothing for the soldiers to divide among themselves: sandals, a robelike garment, a headpiece, a belt, and a tunic. That was the traditional clothing for a Jewish man in Jesus' culture. Evidently the normal arrangement provided for the quaternion charged with guarding a victim to distribute his clothing equally among themselves. If each selected one garment, a fifth garment would remain. Thus according to John, "The soldiers, when they had crucified Jesus, took His garments and made four parts, to each soldier a part, and also the tunic. Now the tunic was without seam, woven from the top in one piece. They said therefore among themselves, "Let us not tear it, but cast lots for it, whose it shall be" (John 19:23–24). The tunic, a fine, woven outer garment, was undoubtedly the best of all the garments, and therefore it was the one they gambled for. Having divided His garments, they sat down to keep watch over Him.

Pilate added to the mockery by having a large placard erected over Jesus' head with the only actual indictment that had been brought against Him. Each of the Gospel writers mentions the sign, but each gives a slightly different variation of what it said. Luke 23:38 and John 19:20

both say that the inscription was written in Greek, Latin, and Hebrew, so the variant readings are easily explained. Either they represent slightly different translations of the inscription or (more likely) they are meant as elliptical restatements of the gist of the full inscription. All accounts agree that the inscription said THE KING OF THE JEWS (Matt. 27:37; Mark 15:26; Luke 23:38; John 19:19).

John says the Sanhedrin was unhappy with the wording, and they wanted the indictment to read, *"He said, 'I am the King of the Jews' "* (John 19:21, emphasis added). But by then, Pilate was tired of playing minion to them, and he told them, "What I have written, I have written" (v. 22).

Read Matthew 27:38-44.

On the chart below, identify the groups of people who mocked Jesus and how they sought to humiliate Him.

Group	How They Humiliated Him
1. _____	_____
2. _____	_____
3. _____	_____

The Greek term for "robbers" signifies that the two criminals crucified with Jesus were no petty thieves but miscreants who lived as outlaws and brigands. They may well have been Barabbas's accomplices, and in that case, the cross on which Christ was crucified would have originally been intended for their leader.

In any case, it is clear that they were the cruelest sort of fellows, because while they hung on their own crosses, each in the throes of his own death agonies, they used what little strength was available to them to taunt Christ, who had never done them harm.

Meanwhile, multitudes were passing by the cross, also hurling insults at the Savior and wagging their heads (vv. 39–40). This was another fulfillment of the array of crucifixion prophecies contained in Psalm 22, where David prophetically describes the cross from the Messiah's own perspective.

Read Psalm 22:6-8. As Jesus hung on the cross, He was:

Feeling _____

Seeing _____

Hearing _____

The mockers around the cross cited the same misunderstanding of Jesus' words recorded in John 2:19 that the false witnesses had used in the trial before Caiaphas. Christ's enemies did not know the prophecy was about to come true, but they persisted in putting a wrong interpretation on His words, and that became the focus of their mockery.

The Sanhedrin was present as well, no doubt inciting much of the mockery. They had come out to the crucifixion site in order to gloat and witness the culmination of their evil plot before they went home to the sanctimonious observance of their Passover meals.

The fact that Jesus hung there dying so helplessly was proof, as far as they were concerned, that He was not who He claimed to be. They announced to everyone, but to no one in particular, "He saved others; Himself He cannot save. If He is the King of Israel, let Him now come down from the cross, and we will believe Him. He trusted in God; let Him deliver Him now if He will have Him" (Matt. 27:42–43). Their words were an almost verbatim fulfillment of the prophecy of Psalm 22:8.

As you read in the margin Isaiah's prophecy of the suffering Jesus would endure, underline what you think caused Him the greatest agony.

Though the abuse and torture men heaped on Him were agony beyond our ability to fathom—those were nothing compared to the wrath of God against the sin He bore.

"But He was pierced through for our transgressions, He was crushed for our iniquities; the chastening for our well-being fell upon Him, and by His scourging we are healed. All of us like sheep have gone astray, each of us has turned to his own way; But the LORD has caused the iniquity of us all to fall on Him" (Isa. 53:5-6 , NASB).

leader Guide

To the Leader:

Contact each person who visited your class today, Easter Sunday, with a note or phone call. Be sure to obtain names and addresses of persons who visited the worship service this Sunday and issue them an invitation to join your class for Bible study.

During the Session

1. Ask: *How do you feel about studying "Murder at Golgotha" on Easter?* State that there can be no Easter joy and victory without first enduring the pain and sorrow of the cross. OR Ask participants what movie portrayals of Jesus' arrest and crucifixion they have seen. Ask: *What was the hardest part of the movie for you to watch? Why? Do you think if you watched the movie several times you'd finally get used to it? Why?*

2. State that the soldiers in charge of Jesus' crucifixion were so hardened by numerous executions they weren't even affected by Jesus' suffering. Complete the first activity of Day 1. Ask: *What was the point of the crown of thorns, robe, and reed?* Discuss participants' responses to the second activity of Day 1. State that Jesus also wore that crown so He could give believers a crown. Direct participants to listen for the kind of crowns Jesus will give His followers as three volunteers read aloud 2 Timothy 4:8; James 1:12; and 1 Peter 5:4. Call for responses. Complete the third activity of Day 1.

3. Use the material in Day 2 to describe how victims of crucifixion were shamed. Discuss the first activity of Day 2. Ask participants to consider the question: *What was the joy that lay before Jesus?* Explain Jesus' greatest joy was bringing salvation to those He loved. Declare: *Jesus bore the shame so you could be with Him for eternity!* Request a volunteer read aloud Mark 15:21. Ask why Mark provided such detail about this man Simon. Remark that Simon and his sons most likely became Christians and were well-known to Mark's readers. (You may refer participants to Paul's greeting to Rufus in Rom. 16:13.) Ask: *What do you think most influenced Simon to put his faith in Christ?*

4. Invite a volunteer to read aloud Matthew 27:33-34. Ask why Jesus refused to drink the sour wine. Discuss the third activity of Day 3. Ask someone to read Psalm 69:19-21. Ask: *How is this psalm prophetic about all we've discussed so far today? How does it make you feel to be given such an intimate look at what Jesus was feeling? How does*

this psalm describe a person who is under a curse? Discuss the first activity of Day 3. Explain that being hung on a tree symbolized God's righteous judgment and His rejection of the sinner. Direct participants to read Galatians 3:13-14 and state why Jesus voluntarily put Himself under God's curse. Explain that Christ took upon Himself all God's judgment for all our sins as well as the curse that was meant for us.

5. Request four volunteers read aloud Matthew 27:35; Mark 15:24; Luke 23:33; and John 19:18. Ask participants why they think each Gospel writer mentioned the actual crucifixion with just one simple statement. Explain that this gruesome form of execution was well-known to the first readers of the Gospels. They were well aware of the pain involved in crucifixion and needed no details. Discuss the last activity in Day 4. Read aloud 1 Peter 2:24 and declare: *Jesus endured such intense pain to heal your pain.*

6. Request that someone read aloud John 19:23-24. Ask why the soldiers' actions were humiliating. Ask a volunteer to read aloud John 19:19-22. Ask whom Pilate intended to humiliate with the sign. Discuss the first activity of Day 5. (Explain you will examine one of the thieves' change of heart in next week's lesson.) State that Dr. MacArthur explained that Psalm 22 describes the cross from Christ's perspective. Discuss the last two activities of Day 5. Request participants give a reason for what they underlined in Isaiah 53:5-6. Direct participants to circle the words *our* and *us* in Isaiah 53:5-6. Ask: *Why did Jesus endure such pain and humiliation?* Declare: *The mockery, the shame, the curse, the pain, and the humiliation was all for* you. *But that's not the end of the story.*

7. Ask someone to read aloud Matthew 28:1-10. Declare that Easter completes Christ's story. Declare that Christ's life is for every person who will accept it. Ask participants to turn to the inside cover of their copies of *MasterWork* and follow along as you explain how to receive forgiveness and new life in Christ. [Don't assume all participants are Christians. Even if they are, this exercise will help them know how to lead others to Christ.] Encourage participants who would like to know more about becoming a Christian to contact you or a church staff member. Close in prayer.

The Seven Last Sayings of Christ

day One

The First Two Sayings

A Plea for Forgiveness

> "When they came to the place called The Skull, there they crucified Him and the criminals, one on the right and the other on the left. But Jesus was saying, 'Father, forgive them; for they do not know what they are doing.' And they cast lots, dividing up His garments among themselves" (Luke 23:33-34 , NASB).

Scripture records seven brief sayings from the Savior on the cross.

The first was a plea for mercy on behalf of His tormentors. Luke records that shortly after the cross was raised on Calvary—while the soldiers were still gambling for His clothing—Jesus prayed to God for forgiveness on their behalf.

Christ responded in precisely the opposite way most men would have. Instead of threatening, lashing back, or cursing His enemies, He prayed to God on their behalf. The phrase "for they do not know what they do" does not suggest that they were unaware that they were sinning. Ignorance does not absolve anyone from sin.

How did Jesus' prayer fulfill the prophecy of Isaiah 53:12?

A Promise of Salvation

Christ's second utterance from the cross marks the first glorious fulfillment of His prayer for His killers' forgiveness, and it shows how generously that forgiveness was bestowed, even on the most unlikely of recipients.

As the hours of agony passed on the cross, one of the two thieves who had mocked Christ earlier had a change of heart. First he rebuked his partner in crime: "Do you not even fear God, seeing you are under the same condemnation? And we indeed justly, for we receive the due reward of our deeds; but this Man has done nothing wrong" (Luke 23:40–41). In saying that much he confessed his own guilt, and he also acknowledged the justice of the penalty he had been given. He affirmed the innocence of Christ as well. Then he turned to Jesus and confessed Him as Lord: "Lord, remember me when You come into Your kingdom" (v. 42). That confession of Jesus as Lord and King was immediately followed by the second of Jesus' seven last sayings: "And Jesus said to him, 'Assuredly, I say to you, today you will be with Me in Paradise' " (v. 43).

That was all Christ said to him. But it was all the thief needed to hear. Realizing that he was in an utterly hopeless situation, the thief sought only a modest token of mercy from Christ: "Remember me." In response no sinner was ever given more explicit assurance of salvation. This incident is one of the greatest biblical illustrations of the truth of justification by faith. This man had done nothing to *merit* salvation. Indeed, he was in no position to do anything meritorious. Already gasping in the throes of his own death agonies, he had no hope of ever *earning* Christ's favor. The Savior at his side was bearing his sin for him. Soon they would be in Paradise together. The thief had Christ's own word on it.

Have you asked Jesus to "be merciful to me a sinner" (Luke 18:13)? ❑ Yes   ❑ No

Have you accepted Jesus' immediate and complete forgiveness of your sins? ❑ Yes   ❑ No

day Two

The Third and Fourth Sayings

A PROVISION FOR HIS MOTHER

Read John 19:25. Who else was at the cross besides Jesus' enemies?

_____

The pain of watching Jesus die must have been agonizing for Jesus' loved ones. But for no one was it more difficult than Mary, His earthly mother. Years before, at His birth, the elderly prophet Simeon had told her, "Behold, this Child is destined for the fall and rising of many in Israel, and for a sign which will be spoken against *(yes, a sword will pierce through your own soul also)*, that the thoughts of many hearts may be revealed" (Luke 2:34–35, emphasis added). The sword Simeon spoke of was now piercing her heart, as she watched her firstborn Son die.

As Mary watched, crowds of people poured contempt on her Son, cruelly mocking and abusing Him. His bleeding, emaciated form hung helplessly on the cross, and all she could do was watch His agony. The sorrow and pain such a sight would cause His mother is unfathomable. And yet instead of shrieking and crumpling in hysteria, turning and fleeing in terror, or falling into a faint at the horrible sight, she stood. She is the very model of courage.

Jesus saw her standing and grieving there, and His third saying from the cross reflects the tender love of a Son for His mother. "When Jesus therefore saw His mother, and the disciple whom He loved standing by, He said to His mother, 'Woman, behold your son!' Then He said to the disciple, 'Behold your mother!' And from that hour that disciple took her to his own home" (John 19:26–27). Jesus was making a gracious provision for Mary in the years to come. He was delegating to John the responsibility to care for Mary in her old age. This was a beautiful gesture, and it says a lot about the personal nature of Jesus' love.

A PETITION TO THE FATHER

Christ's fourth saying from the cross is by far the richest with mystery and meaning.

Read His words printed in the margin.

It might seem at first glance that Christ was merely reciting the words of Psalm 22:1. But given the fact that all of Psalm 22 is an extended prophecy about the crucifixion, it might be better to see the psalm as a prophetic anticipation of the cry of Jesus' heart as He bore the sins of the world on the cross.

"About the ninth hour Jesus cried out with a loud voice, saying, 'ELI, ELI, LAMA SABACHTHANI?' that is, 'MY GOD, MY GOD, WHY HAVE YOU FORSAKEN ME?'" (Matt. 27:46 , NASB).

"My God, my God, why have You forsaken me? Far from my deliverance are the words of my groaning" (Ps. 22:1 , NASB).

As Christ hung there He was bearing the sins of the world. He was dying as a substitute for others. To Him was imputed the guilt of their sins, and He was suffering the punishment for those sins on their behalf. And the very essence of that punishment was the outpouring of God's wrath against sinners. In some mysterious way during those awful hours on the cross, the Father poured out the full measure of His wrath against sin, and the recipient of that wrath was God's own beloved Son!

In this lies the true meaning of the cross. Those who try to explain the atoning work of Christ in any other terms inevitably end up nullifying the truth of Christ's atonement altogether. Scripture teaches this explicitly.

What do each of the following Scripture passages declare happened on that cross?

Romans 8:3 _____

2 Corinthians 5:21 _____

1 Peter 3:18 _____

Jesus received the very same outpouring of divine wrath in all its fury that *we* deserved for our sin. It was a punishment so severe that a mortal man could spend all eternity in the torments of hell, and still he would not have begun to exhaust the divine wrath that was heaped on Christ at the cross.

This was the true measure of Christ's sufferings on the cross. The physical pains of crucifixion—dreadful as they were—were nothing compared to the wrath of the Father against Him. The anticipation of *this* was what had caused Him to sweat blood in the garden. This was why He had looked ahead to the cross with such horror. We cannot begin to fathom all that was involved in paying the price of our sin. It's sufficient to understand that all our worst fears about the horrors of hell—and more—were realized by Him as He received the due penalty of others' wrongdoing.

The Fifth, Sixth, & Seventh Sayings

A PLEADING FOR RELIEF

"After this, Jesus, knowing that all things had already been accomplished, to fulfill the Scripture, said, 'I am thirsty.' A jar full of sour wine was standing there; so they put a sponge full of the sour wine upon a branch of hyssop and brought it up to His mouth" (John 19:28-29 , NASB).

As the end neared, Christ uttered a final plea for physical relief. Earlier He had spat out the vinegar mixed with painkiller that had been offered Him. Now, when He asked for relief from the horrible thirst of dehydration, He was given only a sponge saturated with pure vinegar.

In Jesus' thirst we see the true humanity of Christ. Although He was God incarnate, in His physical body He experienced all the normal human limitations of real human flesh. And none was more vivid than this moment of agonizing thirst after hours of hanging on the cross. And—again, so that the Scriptures might be fulfilled—all He was given to salve His fiery thirst was vinegar. "They also gave me gall for my food, and for my thirst they gave me vinegar to drink" (Ps. 69:21).

A PROCLAMATION OF VICTORY

Read John 19:30. After Jesus received the sour wine He declared, "_____ _____ _____."

In the Greek text this sixth utterance of Jesus from the cross is a single word: *Tetelestai!* Luke 23:46 indicates Jesus made this cry "with a loud voice."

It was a triumphant outcry, full of rich meaning. He did not mean merely that His earthly life was over. He meant that the work the Father had given Him to do was now complete. As He hung there, looking every bit like a pathetic, wasted victim, He nonetheless celebrated the greatest triumph in the history of the universe. Christ's atoning work was finished; redemption for sinners was complete; and He was triumphant.

A PRAYER OF CONSUMMATION

Christ's final saying from the cross was a prayer that expressed the unqualified submission that had been in His heart from the very beginning. Luke records those final words: "And when Jesus had cried out with a loud voice, He said, 'Father, "into Your hands I commit My spirit."' Having said this, He breathed His last" (Luke 23:46).

When Jesus finally expired on the cross, it was not with a wrenching struggle against His killers. He did not display any frenzied death throes. His final passage into death—like every other aspect of the crucifixion drama—was a deliberate act of His own sovereign will, showing that to the very end, He was sovereignly in control of all that was happening. John says, "Bowing His head, He gave up His spirit" (John 19:30). Quietly, submissively, Jesus simply yielded up His life.

Read the Scriptures below and indicate whom you think was ultimately responsible for Jesus' death.

❑ **Wicked people (Acts 2:23)**
❑ **God the Father (Isa. 53:10)**
❑ **No one—Jesus voluntarily gave up His life (John 10:17-18).**
❑ **All of the above**

day *Four*

All Creation Groans, Part 1

Scripture records a number of supernatural phenomena that occurred while Jesus hung on the cross. Those events constituted God's own supernatural commentary on the cross. They are further proof of the extraordinary importance of what was occurring that day just outside Jerusalem.

THE SUN DARKENED

The first of the miraculous signs that accompanied Jesus' death was the darkening of the sky. Matthew writes, "Now from the sixth hour until the ninth hour there was darkness over all the land" (Matt. 27:45). Matthew was counting hours in accord with the Jewish system, so the sixth hour would have been noon. At the moment the noon sun should have been brightest in the sky, a darkness fell over all the land, and remained for three hours. It could not have been an eclipse, because Passover always fell on a full moon, and a solar eclipse would be out of the question during the full moon.

Throughout Scripture, darkness is connected with judgment, and supernatural darkness of this type signifies cataclysmic doom (see Isa. 5:30; Joel 2:2; Amos 5:20; Zeph. 1:14–15).

Read Matthew 27:50-53.

Identify the remarkable miracles that occurred the moment of Christ's death.

1. _____

2. _____

3. _____

THE VEIL TORN

The veil was a heavy curtain that blocked the entrance to the Holy of Holies in the Jerusalem temple, the place where the ark of the covenant was kept, symbolizing the sacred presence of God. Josephus described the veil as ornately decorated, made of blue woven fabric.

Only one person ever traversed the veil, and that was the high priest. He entered the Holy of Holies only once a year, on the Day of Atonement, with the blood of a sacrifice. The veil was of vital symbolic importance, signifying "that the way into the Holiest of All was not yet made manifest" (Heb. 9:8). In other words, it was a constant reminder that sin renders humanity unfit for the presence of God.

The tearing of the curtain at the moment of Jesus' death dramatically symbolized that His sacrifice was a sufficient atonement for sins forever, and the way into the Holy of Holies was now open. The tearing of the high curtain from top to bottom signified that it was God Himself who removed the barrier.

Read Hebrews 4:16. What is the significance for you that the veil was torn?

_____

At the moment the tearing of the veil occurred, the temple was packed with worshipers who were there for the killing of their Passover lambs. By God's design, it was in the very hour that those thousands of lambs were being slain that the true Passover Lamb died. He was the real Lamb whom all the others merely symbolized.

THE EARTH SHAKEN

The Book of Revelation indicates that the final judgment of the earth will commence with a global earthquake more powerful than any ever experienced (see Heb. 12:26–27; Rev. 6:14–15). So it is clear that a supernatural earthquake like this one could only signify the wrath of God. At the cross, the wrath of God against sin was poured out on God's own Son. The accompanying earthquake, coming at the culminating moment of Christ's atoning work, was a kind of divine punctuation mark, perhaps signifying God's anger at the fact that sin had cost His Son so much.

THE DEAD RAISED

The earthquake was evidently powerful enough to split sepulchers. These risen saints most likely came forth from the dead in glorified bodies already fit for heaven (rather than being restored to life in unglorified mortal bodies, as Lazarus had been). They "appeared to many" (Matt. 27:53). Matthew doesn't say what became of the risen saints, but they undoubtedly ascended to glory not long after Jesus' resurrection.

Their appearance proved that Christ had conquered death, not merely for Himself, but for all the saints. This miraculous event prefigured the final great resurrection.

All Creation Groans, Part 2

THE CENTURION SAVED

Perhaps the most important miracle that occurred at the moment of Jesus' death was the conversion of the centurion charged with overseeing the crucifixion. Matthew 27:54 says, "So when the centurion and those with him, who were guarding Jesus, saw the earthquake and the things that had happened, they feared greatly, saying, 'Truly this was the Son of God!' "

Because this particular officer was with those guarding Jesus, it appears he is the very one who had been given charge of overseeing and carrying out the crucifixion of Christ—and probably the crucifixions of the two thieves as well. The words were evidently a true expression of faith. Luke says, *"He glorified God,* saying, 'Certainly this was a righteous Man!'" (Luke 23:47, emphasis added).

THE DRAMA ENDED

John records that as the hour grew late, the Sanhedrin wanted the bodies off the crosses, so that they would not remain there overnight and defile the Sabbath (Deut. 21:23).

> **Read John 19:31-36.**
>
> **What did the Sanhedrin request?** _____
>
> **What did the soldiers do?** _____

The breaking of the legs would make it certain that death would occur almost immediately because once the legs could no longer push up to support the body's weight, the diaphragm would be severely constricted, and air could not be expelled. The victim would die of asphyxiation within minutes. The cruel practice also guaranteed that the victim died with as much pain as possible.

Soldiers from Pilate therefore came to the crucifixion site with the express purpose of breaking the victims' legs.

The soldiers, finding Jesus already dead, decided not to break His bones. Instead, they pierced His side with a spear, to verify that He was dead. The blood and water that flowed out showed that He was. The watery fluid was probably excess serum that had collected in the pericardium (the membrane that encloses the heart).

The soldiers' failure to break Jesus' legs was a further fulfillment of Old Testament prophecy: "He guards all his bones; not one of them is broken" (Ps. 34:20).

Jesus Christ was dead, but death had not conquered Him. On the first day of the week, He would burst forth triumphantly from the grave and show Himself alive to hundreds of eyewitnesses (1 Cor. 15:5–8). The resurrection of Christ was God's stamp of approval on the atonement. Paul wrote that Jesus was "declared to be the Son of God with power according to the Spirit of holiness, by the resurrection from the dead" (Rom. 1:4). The resurrection therefore gave immediate, dramatic, and tangible proof of the efficacy of Christ's atoning death.

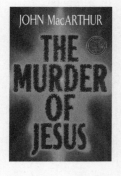

Read Romans 6:8. What is the only way you can share in this miraculous new life of Christ's resurrection?

_____

So, dear friends, don't ever pass over the meaning of the death of Christ on your way to celebrate the resurrection. It is the cross that gives meaning to the resurrection life. Only insofar as we are united with Him in the likeness of His death, can we be certain of being raised with Him in the likeness of His resurrection (Rom. 6:5). That is why "Jesus Christ and Him crucified" remains the very heart and soul of the gospel message.

To the Leader:

When your teaching plan includes numerous Bible references for volunteers to look up and read, write those references on sticky notes and distribute them as participants arrive. That gives participants the opportunity to look up and read over the passages ahead of time and it helps your class time flow more smoothly.

During the Session

1. Ask: *How would you like to die?* Acknowledge that we can't choose the manner in which we'll die (or even IF we'll die, since Jesus may return today!), but we can choose to die with peace and dignity regardless of the circumstances. OR Lead the class to compare the saddest and most joyful funerals they've attended and to determine what made the difference. Acknowledge that death is painful but it doesn't have to be hopeless. FOR EITHER OPTION Declare that Jesus' seven last statements from the cross reveal He remained in control and full of love to the very end. He set the standard for how to live and die.

2. Request a volunteer read aloud Luke 23:33-34. Discuss the first activity of Day 1. State that in the first of Jesus' sayings from the cross we see Jesus interceding for sinners. Ask: *Do you think all those at Golgotha really didn't know what they were doing? What did Jesus mean?* Explain that they were ignorant of the enormity of their crime. Jesus prayed that when those who realized the enormity of their sin repented and sought forgiveness, God would not hold His murder against them. Those who refused to seek forgiveness would not receive it. Direct the class to listen for how Jesus' prayer was answered as volunteers read aloud Acts 2:36-41 and 6:7.

3. State that we see Jesus' prayer for forgiveness answered in His second utterance from the cross. Request someone read aloud Luke 23:39-43. Ask: *What do you think prompted the thief's change of heart? Did he get more than he asked for? Explain. How has Jesus given you far more than you've ever dreamed to ask?*

4. Invite someone to read aloud John 19:25-27. Ask: *If you were Mary, could you have watched Jesus be crucified? Why do you think God chose this woman to be His Son's earthly mother?* Ask why Jesus left His mother's care with John and not with His brothers who are listed in Matthew 13:55. Explain that Jesus' brothers did not believe in Him until after His resurrection (John 7:5; Acts 1:14). Ask: *How does this passage help you appreciate the humanity of Jesus?*

5. Request someone read aloud Matthew 27:46. Ask: *Why would God forsake His own Son? Why is it significant that Jesus cried this out "with a loud voice"?* Explain that Christ's loud voice in His weakened state reveals this was the very outcry of His soul. Remark that Jesus went to the depths of despair so we would never have to. Discuss how people should respond to that truth.

6. Ask someone to read aloud John 19:28-29. Inquire: *What is painful to you about this episode? Why did we need to know Jesus was thirsty?* Ask someone to read aloud John 4:14. Declare that Jesus experienced thirst so we would never have to. Invite volunteers to share how Jesus has satisfied their thirst. Discuss the first activity of Day 3. Discuss: *What did Jesus mean by this cry humanly and theologically?* Request someone read aloud Luke 23:44-46. Discuss the last activity of Day 3.

7. Ask: *Why did it get dark?* Point out that the natural world reacted as the Light of the world faded. Complete the first activity of Day 4. Direct participants to use the material in Day 4 to state the significance of each miraculous event.

8. Invite three volunteers to read aloud Matthew 27:54; Mark 15:39; and Luke 23:47. State that it is likely that this centurion had been in charge of the military detail that had handled Jesus from His arrest to His crucifixion. Direct the class to describe all the centurion had seen in the past 18 hours. Ask: *What do you think most influenced him to declare, "This was the Son of God"?* Note that the centurion's profession of faith is another answer to Jesus' prayer in Luke 23:34. Invite two volunteers to read aloud John 19:31-34 and Mark 15:43-44. Ask: *Why is it significant that Jesus died earlier than they expected?* Declare Jesus was sovereign even over the timing of His death.

9. Inquire: *Has this study of "The Murder of Jesus" been a pleasant experience for you? Why? What part of Christ's passion impacted you the most? Why? Why shouldn't we just skip over Jesus' gruesome death and focus on His glorious resurrection?* Discuss the last activity of Day 5. Ask: *How can we die with Christ so we can live?*

10. Announce the new study from Tony Evans's *Life Essentials* that begins next week.

11. Close in prayer.

ABOUT THE WRITERS

Tony Evans

is the senior pastor of Oak Cliff Bible Fellow-ship and president of The Urban Alternative, a national ministry that equips the church to promote clear understanding and relevant application of Scripture to urban communities. He is the author of numerous books, including *The Promise, What Matters Most, Returning to Your First Love, The Battle Is the Lord's,* and *Free at Last.*

AMY SUMMERS wrote the personal learning activities and teaching plans for this unit. Amy is an experienced writer for LifeWay Bible study curriculum, a wife, a mother, and a Sunday School leader from Arden, North Carolina. She is a graduate of Baylor University and Southwestern Baptist Theological Seminary (M.R.E.).

ABOUT THIS STUDY

"We are to grow up in all aspects into Him, who is the head, even Christ" (Eph. 4:15).

According to Ephesians 4:15, what is God's desire for us?

_____

If that is your desire as well, ask God to use this study to help you experience maximum spiritual growth.

Life Essentials

for Knowing God *Better*, Experiencing God *Deeper*, Loving God *More*

One day I was walking through my yard with a workman who was going to cut down and remove some dead trees. I showed him one tree I wanted him to cut down because it appeared dead to me.

"Oh, sir," he said quickly, "you don't need to cut this tree down. It's still alive." Then he proceeded to show me some small green buds on the tree that I had not noticed. What looked like death to me was really stunted growth. Because this tree had not been properly nurtured and developed, it appeared to have no life at all.

Countless Christians today are like that underdeveloped tree. At first glance they may appear to have no spiritual life at all, but upon closer observation their problem is seen to be severely retarded development. Because of their lack of spiritual growth, too many Christians are not experiencing the abundant life Jesus promised .

This study is about spiritual growth. If you have truly trusted the Lord Jesus Christ to be your Sin-bearer, and you are looking to Him alone for forgiveness and the gift of eternal life, then you have life abiding in you. What is needed now is more growth, not more life.

The problem, however, is that many Christians either don't know how spiritual growth occurs or they are refusing to allow it to occur. My goal is to motivate and educate you in the essential elements of spiritual growth so you can grow into a mature spiritual adult, one who consistently lives under the lordship of Jesus Christ.

Spiritual growth is guaranteed to every true believer. No child of God has to remain stagnant and spiritually underdeveloped. In the pages to follow, you will discover how to cooperate with God's grace in order to experience maximum spiritual growth.

It is my hope that this study will incite and excite you to pursue the full experience of your life in Christ and discover the joy of being transformed into the image of God's Son.

Beginning the Process

The Importance of Spiritual Growth

THE NECESSITY OF SPIRITUAL GROWTH

Getting a handle on spiritual growth is crucial. First, it is God's command and, therefore, His will for us. And second, the alternative to growth is stagnation and eventual deformity. Failing to grow is not an option for believers—at least not if we want to please God.

Spiritual growth demands nourishment. "Like newborn babies, long for the pure milk of the word, so that by it you may grow in respect to salvation" (1 Pet. 2:2). This is one of the best one-sentence descriptions of spiritual growth you'll find in the Bible.

Spiritual growth also demands relationship. A baby is dependent on other people for the nourishment needed for proper growth. This begins even before birth as an unborn child draws nourishment from the mother. If that relationship is disrupted, the baby is in serious trouble.

The spiritual application of this physical truth is the importance of our relationship with Jesus Christ. Jesus said, "I came that they may have life, and have it abundantly" (John 10:10). Spiritual growth is progressively learning to let Christ live His life through us, and that only happens by relationship.

THE INGREDIENTS FOR SPIRITUAL GROWTH

Since this session is an overview and introduction to our subject, I'm hitting the highlights as we talk about the importance of spiritual growth.

Read 2 Peter 3:18 below and underline the two ingredients of spiritual growth.

"Grow in the grace and knowledge of our Lord and Savior Jesus Christ. To Him be the glory, both now and to the day of eternity. Amen" (2 Pet. 3:18).

Spiritual growth is "that transformational process by which we allow the indwelling Christ to increasingly express Himself in and through us, resulting in a greater capacity on our part to bring God greater glory and experience His greater good for ourselves. … Spiritual growth is more of Christ being expressed in my life through less of me."
—Tony Evans

Grace is all that God is free to do for you based on the work of Jesus Christ on your behalf. It is God's inexhaustible supply of goodness whereby He does for you what you could never do for yourself.

Peter told us to grow in the *knowledge* of Jesus Christ. Our goal is to know Christ, not just know about Him. Knowledge is an ingredient of spiritual growth, but it is knowledge of a person we must seek.

> "Our goal is to know Christ, not just know about Him."—Tony Evans

If you are serious about spiritual growth, the driving force must be pursuing a living relationship with Christ, which deepens as you get to know Him better.

Read Philippians 3:10. Indicate on the scale below how closely your life's goal resembles Paul's.

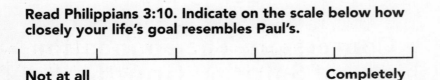

Not at all   **Completely**

THE PRODUCT OF SPIRITUAL GROWTH

God takes His glory very seriously, which is why He wants you to seek Him and know Him and grow in Him, not just because it's the right thing to do but because you want to be a person through whom He can express Himself and display His magnificent glory.

Many Christians are not growing, even though they desire a closer relationship with Christ and are doing things to facilitate this relationship. Their emphasis is on them and what they are doing instead of focusing on God and His glory.

When we glorify God, we are saying He is a person of great value. Glorifying God means we draw attention to Him and promote Him as worthy of all praise and adoration. We glorify God when we reflect the light of His character the way the moon reflects the brilliance of the sun.

According to 2 Corinthians 3:18, what will happen when you focus on glorifying God?

_____

THE BENEFITS OF SPIRITUAL GROWTH

So what's in this for you and me if we commit ourselves to grow God's way? Jesus said, "Seek first [God's] kingdom and His righteousness, and all these things will be added to you" (Matt. 6:33). God will meet the needs of His children.

Even when things happen that don't seem to be good for us, God is at work shaping and growing us. God has a good purpose in everything He allows into our lives. If you will take care of the business of pursuing and glorifying God, He will take care of your growth, freeing you to enjoy all the rights and privileges of this new relationship.

day *Two*

Conversion: The Foundation of Spiritual Growth

Conversion is the foundation of our spiritual growth. You can't build a solid structure on a partial or faulty foundation, so I want to lay a solid foundation for spiritual growth by discussing our complete need for conversion, the character of conversion, and the completeness of the new life and new nature God placed within us when we trusted Christ for salvation.

To understand and appreciate what God did for us at conversion and its implications for our spiritual growth, we need to see it against the backdrop of the sinful nature we had before coming to Christ.

THE NECESSITY OF CONVERSION

When Adam sinned against God, his innocence was lost and he became corrupted by sin. At the core of Adam's being there was deposited a sin nature, which became a part of his humanity and was transmitted to every one of his descendants. The Bible says, "Through one man sin entered into the world, and death through sin" (Rom. 5:12). Because Adam was acting as the representative head of the human race when he sinned, all of us are born with a disposition toward rebellion against God that is part of what it means to be human.

Our problem as people born in sin is not that we have a minor flaw that needs to be ironed out or a quirk of personality that we ought to work on. Sin sets us at complete hostility toward God and puts us under His judgment. Paul stated it succinctly: "Those who are in the flesh cannot please God" (Rom. 8:8).

The Bible declares that every person is born with a short circuit in his spiritual nerve system. God is sending out His signals, but the unsaved person has no capacity to receive them (see 1 Cor. 2:14).

There can be no growth where a new spiritual birth has not taken place. That may be obvious to you, but there are legions of people who go to church every week and consider themselves Christians yet never exhibit any spiritual growth. They think they are doing all the right things yet they wonder why their religion seems so empty and unsatisfying.

Look up John 3:7. What does Jesus say to each person who strives to please God with religious activity?

"A natural man does not accept the things of the Spirit of God, for they are foolishness to him; and he cannot understand them, because they are spiritually appraised" (1 Cor. 2:14).

THE CHARACTER OF CONVERSION

God Gives Us His Nature at Conversion

Conversion, or salvation, or the new birth, is the process whereby God deposits within every believer a new nature that is from Him and is therefore perfect. The old nature has been put to death, and in its place is a new nature from God that the Bible says cannot sin (see 1 John 3:9). That doesn't mean we are perfect. We still bear the residue of the old sin nature. It is just that sin no longer is operating as the essence of who we are.

When you receive Christ, everything becomes new at the core of your being, and it is this new life or new nature that gives you the disposition and the capacity to know and serve God rather than serving sin and self.

"No one who is born of God practices sin, because His seed abides in him; and he cannot sin, because he is born of God" (1 John 3:9).

Read 2 Peter 1:3-4. What is the new nature God gives believers?_____

What has God given to enable you to nurture that new nature? _____

Our New Nature Needs to Be Nurtured

If you are a genuine believer, that new nature from God is there. This new nature may be buried under old ways of thinking and acting, but it's there

"If anyone is in Christ, he is a new creature; the old things passed away; behold, new things have come" (2 Cor. 5:17).

and it needs to be nurtured. Spiritual growth is the process of nurturing and developing the new nature that God implanted in your heart, at the deepest core of your being.

The miracle of the new birth is that this transformation and growth occurs in the midst of and in spite of our flawed humanity. Christians still struggle with sin, and we will continue to struggle until Jesus comes and gives us new bodies. God is not interested in just trying to knock the dents out of our old sinful self, sand down the rough places, and give our flesh a fresh coat of paint.

Our Old Self Is a Total Loss

Too many of us are busy trying to repair the old nature and make it look new when God is in the business of throwing out the old and crafting something brand-new.

God has declared our old nature a total loss because we were born in sin. He wants us to concentrate on the new nature He has given us. If you have spent years trying to fix up what God says cannot be fixed up, then I hope the truth of God's Word and the message of this study will liberate you from a frustrating way of life.

day *Three*

Conversion

THE COMPLETENESS OF CONVERSION

We're driving home the importance of conversion as the foundation of spiritual growth because that's where the Bible locates our growth. It's also important to grasp these truths because this subject is surrounded by so much confusion and misunderstanding among Christians.

You Have All You Need to Grow

God deposited more in you at your salvation than you could ever imagine. You have everything you need to grow and become spiritually mature because you have the Holy Spirit living inside you and because of the work God has done in your heart and mind.

As you read Hebrews 10:14-17 printed in the margin, underline what God has done in your heart and mind. What is the significance of that?

_____

God says that He is doing something new with His people under the new covenant, which is described in Jeremiah 31:31-34 and from which the writer of Hebrews was quoting. Under the old covenant, God wrote His laws on tablets of stone—but the people lacked the internal power to keep those laws. Under the new covenant, God writes His laws on the hearts and minds of His people, which means He gives us both the desire (through our hearts) and the power (through our minds) to obey and please Him (see Rom. 7:22).

"By one offering He has perfected for all time those who are sanctified. And the Holy Spirit also testifies to us; for after saying, 'THIS IS THE COVENANT THAT I WILL MAKE WITH THEM AFTER THOSE DAYS, SAYS THE LORD: I WILL PUT MY LAWS UPON THEIR HEART, AND ON THEIR MIND I WILL WRITE THEM,' He then says, 'AND THEIR SINS AND THEIR LAWLESS DEEDS I WILL REMEMBER NO MORE' " (Heb. 10:14-17).

You'll Have a New Struggle

Having a new heart and mind means you get an entirely new set of tastes, attitudes, and desires that are directed toward God. And when these new things come into contact with your old sinful flesh, conflict is inevitable.

Paul wrote very candidly about this conflict in Romans 6–8. Read Romans 7:15-17, printed in the margin. Does this sound familiar? What Paul discovered is that when he came to Christ, his entire orientation to life changed. Now that he had God's law written on his heart, he could not sin without feeling his new nature coming against that sin and constantly drawing him back to Christ.

"What I am doing, I do not understand; for I am not practicing what I would like to do, but I am doing the very thing I hate. But if I do the very thing I do not want to do, I agree with the Law, confessing that the Law is good. So now, no longer am I the one doing it, but sin which dwells in me" (Rom. 7:15-17).

You'll Have New Appetites

This new heart we received at salvation manifests itself in new spiritual desires or appetites (see Heb. 10:14-16). Your new nature craves intimacy and fellowship with God, and it desires to please and obey Him more than anything else. These are intense cravings, which is why you can't sin as a Christian and enjoy it or feel no remorse for it the way you did when you were an unbeliever.

When you feed your new, God-given appetites, you enjoy the immense satisfaction of His blessing and you begin to grow spiritually. God's law that is written on your heart becomes the most real and vital thing operating in your life, and you are able to bring more areas of your life under the lordship of Christ. In the process you'll also have a new desire to glorify God.

It's What's on the Inside That Counts

When it's all said and done, spiritual growth does not primarily depend on what is happening around you but on what is happening inside of you. Growth comes from the inside out, which is the way God designed all of His creation to function.

Spiritual growth is the process of expanding and releasing what is on the inside so that it becomes visible on the outside. What God often does is apply heat and pressure to bring about this release. That's why our greatest times of spiritual growth are almost always our times of greatest trial.

> **Read Galatians 5:16. Have you been striving to:**
> ❑ **Control your outer behavior so you can be Spirit-filled?**
> ❑ **Allow the Spirit to fill and lead you so your outer behavior changes?**

Lasting spiritual growth comes about through internal transformation, not just external reformation. The Holy Spirit working on the inside produces spiritual victory on the outside. All we need to walk in victory and grow in Christ is already present within us.

day *Four*

Identity: The Key to Spiritual Growth

When I used to take my children to the circus, we would go outside before the show to see the elephants. These huge animals weighing several tons each were kept in place by a single chain wrapped around one foot and tied to a small stake. Any one of those elephants could have easily ripped that stake out of the ground and run away, but that almost never happened because circus elephants have been conditioned to submit when they feel the tug of that chain on their legs.

Much like elephants in the circus, a lot of Christians are being held hostage by a small chain that holds them down and keeps them from getting anywhere. These people go to church and hear about the power and spiritual authority God has for them as believers in Jesus Christ, but they can't seem to kick free of the chains holding them in bondage. What people in this condition need is to understand who they are in Christ.

A person's identity is a critical commodity. Having a clear identity is so important to our human makeup that some people go to great lengths to try to gain an identity they think will make them acceptable. A good portion of commerce in the Western world is geared toward helping people look, feel, and act as something other than what they really are, because someone has convinced them there is something wrong with their true identity.

Another common mistake people make is linking their identity with their activity. We do this when we identify ourselves by our profession or trade. Confusing what we do with our real identity is an easy mistake to make, but the confusion is still lethal if we want to grow and thrive in our daily walk with the Lord.

What things do you allow to influence your identity? Circle all that apply.

Career   Children   Talents   Possessions

Activities   Appearance   Other: _____

OUR IDENTITY BEGINS AT THE CROSS

When God gave you a new nature, He put to death your old nature. This death occurred on the cross of Jesus Christ, when He died for the sins of the world. This is why your identity as a Christian begins at the cross.

The truth of this is expressed so clearly in Galatians 2:20. Read that verse in the margin. If you can absorb and apply what the Bible teaches in this passage, you are well on your way to growing spiritually.

> "I have been crucified with Christ; and it is no longer I who live, but Christ lives in me; and the life which I now live in the flesh I live by faith in the Son of God, who loved me and gave Himself up for me" (Gal. 2:20).

We Died with Christ

"I have been crucified with Christ." To be crucified is to die. We know that Jesus died on the cross, but His death also brought about the death of the sin nature of those who are identified with Him. Because that's true, we had better be looking for our identity somewhere else, since dead people don't grow. Too many believers aren't growing because they are still hanging out in the cemetery with the corpse of their old self, trying to resuscitate what God has put to death.

Our Death Is Spiritual

You may be saying, "I didn't feel like I died when I got saved." According to Romans 6:11, how can you make this spiritual death real in your life?

_____

If God has pronounced your old self dead, why would you want to mess around with that corpse and live in the realm of death when He has a new life for you? God wants you to leave the cemetery of the old life and take up your new identity as His child.

Read the passages below and note what you received with your new identity.

1 Corinthians 2:16: _____

Ephesians 2:6: _____

We now have the capacity to think God's thoughts. This new mind also includes our emotions, desires, attitudes, and all of the other components that make up the core of our being.

We also have a new location. When Christ raised us from the dead, He raised us all the way. After Christ was resurrected, He ascended back into heaven and is seated "at [God's] right hand in the heavenly places" (Eph. 1:20). Everything that happened to Christ in His death, burial, and resurrection happened to us spiritually.

Identity

CHRIST HAS BECOME OUR LIFE

Our identification with Christ is so complete that Paul could say, "It is no longer I who live, but *Christ lives in me*" (Gal. 2:20, italics added). The most fundamental truth of the Christian life is that Jesus Christ takes up residence within us when we receive Him as Savior. But Galatians 2:20 is saying more than that in terms of our identity as believers. It is not just that Christ is in us, but that He is *living* in us.

Christ does not just want to dwell in us. He wants to move in and settle down and fully express Himself through our lives. Allowing Christ to live out His life through us is the fountainhead of spiritual growth, for only God working in us by the power of the Holy Spirit can produce lasting growth and change in us.

A lot of Christians who are going to heaven are not growing in Christ here on earth because they are not allowing Him to be fully at home in their hearts. These people treat Christ the way we treat our guests. What we mean by "Make yourself at home" is, "Stay here in this one room and don't mess with anything else."

In order for Jesus Christ to make Himself at home in your heart, He needs to have the run of the house. We're talking about the contrast between just living and being alive.

Is Christ ❑ a guest or ❑ the ruler in your heart?

Jesus is the only person who has ever lived the Christian life successfully—and He offers to live His life in you! God never asked you to be a Christian in your own power. But He does expect you to yield your body to Christ as a living sacrifice (see Rom. 12:1) so He can express His perfect love, power, and holiness through you. That's what it means to be identified with Christ.

According to 1 Corinthians 1:30, what do you have when you are in Christ and He lives in you?

_____

When you received Christ, you got the whole package. He is your reference point and identity. Through Jesus, there is nothing you cannot do (see Matt. 19:26).

Give me the fingers of Mozart, and there is no musical piece I cannot play. Give me the mind of Einstein, and there is no mathematical formula I cannot unravel. Give me the arms of Hank Aaron, and there is no home run I cannot hit. Give me the life of Jesus Christ, and there is no victory I cannot achieve.

"Jesus said to them, 'With men this is impossible, but with God all things are possible.' " (Matt. 19:26).

CHRIST IS LIVING THROUGH YOU

The Christian life is not a passive relationship in which we sit back and cruise along while Jesus Christ does all the work. The new life we received from God operates through our bodies and our personalities. We must work in cooperation with Christ's work in us. He can supply all that is needed, but not apart from our will and our mind.

The problem Paul struggled with in Romans 6–8 is that while he agreed that God's law was perfect and good, he found himself unable to pull off the good things he knew he should be doing. Paul had to come to grips with the fact that it wasn't him trying his best to obey God, but it was Christ *in him* that gave him power over sin.

Look at Galatians 2:20 again (p. 99). What phrase explains how you can live this new life where Christ expresses Himself through you?

_____

The Christian life is lived by faith in Christ, but this faith is not a cold academic exercise. The last part of Galatians 2:20 reminds us that Christ "loved me and gave Himself up for me." Jesus wants you to trust Him, but not the way you trust your bank to take care of your money or your car to get you where you're going. Living by faith is cultivating a relationship with the living Christ who wants you to identify with Him so closely that people can't tell you apart. You've never been loved like this before.

Our new identity in Christ solves the problem of acceptance because when you understand who you are in Christ, you realize you have already been accepted by the God of the universe, and no one can improve on that.

So who are you? You are a totally forgiven, fully accepted, absolutely loved child of God. That is your new identity in Jesus Christ, and once you come to grips with the reality of it you will be ready to grow like you have never grown before.

"Living by faith is cultivating a relationship with the living Christ who wants you to identify with Him so closely that people can't tell you apart."
—Tony Evans

Before the Session

Gather several unpopped and popped kernels of popcorn. (Step 6)

During the Session

1. Ask: *Have you ever told someone to grow up? What did you mean by that?* OR If your class is comprised of parents, ask them to list the greatest difficulties and joys of being a parent. Ask: *What kept you going through feedings, toddler tantrums, and teenage attitudes?* Remind everyone that we can handle difficult phases by understanding our children will grow out of them! Growth is the expected outcome of every birth. God expects His children to grow. FOR EITHER OPTION Explain that this study will explore what God means when He tells us to grow up. Use the introduction on page 91 to share Dr. Evans's goal for this study.

2. Explain: *Week 1 states the importance, foundation, and key to spiritual growth.* Ask a volunteer to read the definition of spiritual growth in the margin of Day 1 (p. 92). Invite someone to read John 3:26-30. Explore how John the Baptist expressed the essence of spiritual growth. Ask participants for two reasons Dr. Evans said spiritual growth is necessary [God's command; alternative is stagnation and eventual deformity].

3. Ask the class to compare what a baby and a believer need to develop properly. Discuss the first activity of Day 1 (p. 92). Ask for volunteers to read Ephesians 2:8 and Colossians 2:6. Ask: *How did we receive Christ? How are we to walk in Him?* Explain that God tells us what we need to do to grow and His grace helps us do it. Ask what kind of knowledge is involved in spiritual growth. Inquire: *How do you get to know someone? Is initial knowledge enough? Do you ever quit getting to know your spouse, children, friends? Why? What must be your driving force if you're really serious about spiritual growth?*

4. Ask what the product of spiritual growth is to be. Explore what it means to glorify God. Explain that if we're going to grow spiritually we must change our focus from ourselves to God's glory. Discuss the final activity in Day 1 (p. 93). Remind members that being transformed into Christ's

There may be people in your class who have attended church all their lives but never committed to a personal relationship with the Lord. Pray this lesson will speak powerfully to each learner in every stage of spiritual development. Be sensitive to opportunities to guide participants to make that faith commitment.

image is just one of many benefits of spiritual growth. Ask them to share other benefits of spiritual growth.

5. Ask learners to share the foundation of spiritual growth. Ask someone to read the final paragraph under "The Necessity of Conversion" (p. 95). Discuss the activity that follows. Ask what you receive when you're born again. Discuss the final activity of Day 2. Ask: *If you totaled your car and were given a new car, would you keep trying to fix the old one? Why?* Explain that we must quit trying to fix the old nature and work on developing our new nature.

6. Talk about the first activity of Day 3 (p. 97). Ask what same basic truth is stated in 2 Peter 1:3-4. [God has given us everything we need to grow.] Discuss what believers receive when they get a new heart and mind. Encourage participants not to be discouraged by inner struggles against sin—that's proof they are growing. Display the popcorn kernels. Explain that heat causes steam to build up inside the kernel. The shell finally breaks under the pressure and releases the corn inside. Explore how popcorn illustrates the spiritual growth process.

7. Ask why Dr. Evans said identity is the key to spiritual growth. Ask participants to share what they learn about their identity from Galatians 2:20. Discuss the last activity in Day 4 (p. 100). Read the paragraph following that activity. Ask: *If our identity is in Christ, what kind of mind do we have, and where do we really live? What difference does this make?*

8. Ask where Christ lives if our identity is in Him. Explore the significance of the truth that Christ lives in believers. Ask: *Why would Dr. Evans say, "Give me the life of Jesus Christ and there is no victory I cannot achieve"?* Discuss the final activity of Day 5. Explain: *By grace we receive salvation and growth and by faith we live it out everyday.* Discuss what it means to live by faith. Remind learners that spiritual growth is not a program but a relationship with a loving God. Ask someone to read the final paragraph of Day 5. Discuss why grasping your identity in Christ will free you up to grow. Close in prayer.

Sin, Grace, and Faith

day One

Sin: The Hindrance to Spiritual Growth

Dwarfism is a condition that results in stunted growth because something in the victim's body blocks or restricts production of the human growth hormone that is vital to normal development.

There is a parallel to dwarfism in the spiritual realm that can also result in stunted growth. We seem to have a generation of spiritual dwarfs today who are failing to reach their full spiritual potential and maximum maturity in Christ. There may be many individual reasons for this, but we have to come back to the fact that sin in its myriad forms and manifestations is the biggest hindrance to spiritual growth.

SIN ALWAYS SEPARATES US FROM GOD

The sin that hinders growth and fellowship in the life of a Christian is a different issue from the sin that separated us from God as unbelievers. We are addressing sin that contaminates the life of a believer and hinders communion with God and usefulness for Him. Those who are outside of Christ must deal with the sin that condemns a person to eternal separation from God.

The day is coming when Jesus will deliver us not only from sin's power, but from its very presence. Until then we must deal with sin, but we have a powerful ally in God's grace. As grace flows to us and through us, it stimulates the growth of our new nature.

Read Galatians 5:17. Describe the struggle that goes on inside a believer.

_____

_____

We still struggle with sin because our new nature is living in the old house of our sin-contaminated flesh. The good news is that the new nature is now in the dominant place of influence and control.

The more you grow spiritually, the more the Spirit dominates the flesh rather than the flesh defeating us and thwarting the Spirit's work in our lives. Sin will stunt your growth by restricting the flow of God's grace and power.

GOD CANNOT TOLERATE SIN

"This is the message we have heard from Him and announce to you, that God is Light, and in Him there is no darkness" (1 John 1:5). No darkness, sin, or evil can exist in the perfect light of God's presence. Since no sin at all can exist in His light, we have to realize that our sin even as believers creates a barrier between us and a God who is absolutely pure. God will never adjust to the darkness. If unconfessed sin is present in our lives, His presence is absent.

"God will never adjust to the darkness. If unconfessed sin is present in our lives, His presence is absent." —Tony Evans

God is omnipresent in His deity, which means we cannot go anyplace where He is not. But fellowship with Him is only found in the light. Our problem is that we can and do adjust to the darkness. If you step out of the light into a dark room or go outside on a dark night, you know that if you stay there long enough your eyes will make the necessary adjustments.

Read 1 John 1:6. If you claim to have fellowship with God but allow sin to exist unchecked in your life, you:

_____

If you are walking in the darkness, you are walking alone. God doesn't show up when you are hanging out in the neighborhood of sin.

According to 1 John 1:7, what is your alternative to

walking in the dark? _____

What do you think it means to walk in the light?

_____

Walking in the light means you see your sin as God sees it so you can do something about it. Rather than trying to cover up or deny sin, spiritual people who are growing in grace are constantly becoming more aware of how unlike God they are. The darkness in us is most fully exposed when we come into the pure light of God's holy presence. The closer you draw to God, the more aware of sin you become.

Sin and Grace

WE NEED TO CONFESS OUR SIN TO GOD

We have two choices when it comes to the sin that cuts off the free flow of God's grace and stunts our spiritual growth. We can cover it or confess it.

Read Psalm 32:3-6 and 1 John 1:8-9. Note the results of:

Choosing to cover your sin: _____

Choosing to confess your sin: _____

Allowing your sin to be exposed is a good thing, even though it may feel bad for a while. When you start feeling convicted because of something that is not right in your life, it means the Holy Spirit has shined the light on a problem so it can be corrected.

A lot of us treat our sins the way we treat our laundry, letting them pile up and then dealing with them all at once. But the Holy Spirit doesn't follow our schedule. His conviction of sin is often instantaneous. The minute those words went out of our mouths, we knew we shouldn't have said them. The time to confess and be cleansed of that sin is the moment we are aware of it.

In terms of our eternal standing before God, our forgiveness occurred at the cross. That was a judicial act that brought us into right standing with God for eternity. Forgiving our sins as Christians is a relational act that keeps us in close fellowship with God every day.

Confession allows us to override sin by triggering God's forgiveness so that the flow of grace continues. And when grace flows, growth follows.

GRACE: THE ENVIRONMENT OF SPIRITUAL GROWTH

We love to sing songs about God's grace, but growing in grace each day is often another story. Why is this so hard to do? One reason is that grace is a foreign environment to us. The Bible says we have to grow in grace because it is outside of our normal orientation.

A failure to understand and grow in grace inevitably results in faulty development and stunted spiritual growth. We were born in sin, not in grace. No one had to show us how to act out our sinful nature, but we will spend the rest of our lives learning what it means to live by grace.

Grace is the inexhaustible supply of God's goodness whereby He does for you what you could never do for yourself. Grace gives you for free what you do not deserve, could not earn, and would never be able to repay.

"Grace gives you for free what you do not deserve, could not earn, and would never be able to repay."
—Tony Evans

WE WERE DEAD WITHOUT GOD'S GRACE

Sometimes we need to look back and remember where we were before we can appreciate where we are today. Your appreciation of grace will soar, and your spiritual growth will be helped when you see where God brought you from.

Read Ephesians 2:1-3 and fill in the blanks.

Before I was saved by God's grace,

I was _____

I walked _____

I lived_____

and I was by nature _____

If you have ever shopped for a diamond or other precious stone, you know that the jeweler places the stone on black velvet to make it shine more brilliantly and enhance its beauty. Verses 1-3 of Ephesians 2 are the dark background against which Paul is about to show us the grace of God.

Paul summed up our hopeless condition by saying we were "dead" in sin. The Bible is talking about spiritual death here and not necessarily physical death, although physical death is the natural consequence of sin. But since the death spoken of here is spiritual, most people don't grasp its reality as readily as they do the reality of physical death.

A lot of spiritually dead people don't feel dead. And as far as they and the people around them are concerned, they don't look dead. But those who are still in their sins are dead, according to God's Word.

Whether you go out in a pine box or a beautiful coffin, you're still dead. When you were dead in your sins, you were cut off from the eternal life Christ gives. And the only alternative to eternal life is eternal death, which means eternal separation from God and the suffering of hell.

day Three

Grace and Faith

GOD'S GRACE HAS MADE US ALIVE IN CHRIST

Ephesians 2:4 begins with two of the most important, exciting, and life-changing words in the Bible: "But God" are words that will reverse any situation. "But God" will bring life where death existed because of what God has done for us in grace.

According to Ephesians 2:4-5, what has God done for

you by His grace? _____

"By grace you have been saved." That last phrase is the key here. If you know Christ as your Savior, you are saved not because of your decision or anything else you did but because God took the initiative to reach down and save you by grace.

My friend, grace is God's kindness and gentleness to us when He could have backed us into a corner as guilty sinners and destroyed us without violating His holy character. But God wanted to make us His children, so instead of expressing His wrath against us, He poured it out on His own sinless Son on the cross. Jesus took our punishment so God could embrace us. We have a brand-new relationship with God through grace.

After making us alive with Christ when we were dead, God took us to heaven with Jesus when He rose from the dead and ascended back to His place at God's right hand.

"[God] raised us up with Him, and seated us with Him in the heavenly places in Christ Jesus" (Eph. 2:6). God takes those people He has saved and by that same grace seats them with Christ in what the Bible calls "the heavenly places." God "raised" us up and "seated" us with Christ, past tense. It has already been done. You may be living on earth, but your true existence is in heaven, where the Bible says you are already seated with Christ.

Think of all God has blessed you with on earth, and then try to imagine what His kindness will be like when all the limitations of earth—including sin—are removed. God's grace will just keep flowing in a never-ending stream, and no two gifts will be alike because He is infinite.

The moment you came to Christ, God brought you back from the dead and seated you with Jesus Christ in heaven. Your eternal future is secure, because heaven is included in the package called God's grace.

GOD'S GRACE IS SUPER ABUNDANT FOR OUR NEEDS

God will always relate to you in grace, and He has all the grace you need. But it is grace related to your need. You don't get tomorrow's grace today. You don't get dying grace until you're dying. You don't get grace to face temptation until you're being tempted.

What most people really want to know is, *If God is so gracious, why doesn't He just take away the trial or the suffering? Why doesn't He keep the thorns from growing in our lives instead of giving us the grace to endure them?*

"God is able to make all grace abound to you, so that always having all sufficiency in everything, you may have an abundance for every good deed" (2 Cor. 9:8).

Paul had "a thorn in the flesh, a messenger of Satan to torment me—to keep me from exalting myself!" (2 Cor. 12:7). Paul's thorn could have been a physical problem, a person who caused him grief, or a problem with no solution. Whatever it was, God allowed it to keep Paul humble and to teach him a valuable lesson.

Read 2 Corinthians 12:9. What lesson did God want

Paul to learn? _____

Do you believe God's grace is enough for whatever you're facing? ❑ Yes ❑ No ❑ I'm getting there.

So the question that needs to be asked is from God to us, not us to God. His question to us is, "Do you want to see My grace operating in super-abundant power in your life?"

If your answer is, "Yes, Lord, more than anything," then be ready to accept the thorns He puts in your path. When problems come, it means God is getting ready to show you more of His grace, because where He's taking you is greater than where you are now. All you need to know is that His grace is sufficient.

OUR RESPONSE TO GOD'S GRACE

Ephesians 2:8-10 teaches us that anything we could possibly do for God is simply a response of gratitude to His grace, not a payment for it.

Grace should not lead us to try to take advantage of God's goodness by sinning all we want or by doing nothing while soaking up His favor. God has work for us to do, but He doesn't want us serving Him because we're trying to pay Him back and earn our own way. That is working against grace. God wants us to serve Him in response to His relationship with us, which is a relationship of love and grace. Grace means that we make ourselves available to God for Him to do something through us.

Why have you been doing good works?
❏ **to earn God's grace**
❏ **in response to God's grace working in you**

"By grace you have been saved through faith; and that not of yourselves, it is the gift of God; not as a result of works, so that no one may boast. For we are His workmanship, created in Christ Jesus for good works, which God prepared beforehand so that we would walk in them" (Eph. 2:8-10).

Faith: The Action of Spiritual Growth

Faith is the mechanism God has given us whereby we can tap into the spiritual realm that is above and beyond the world of our five senses. So crucial is living by faith to the process of knowing and experiencing God that without it spiritual growth is impossible.

THE MEANING OF FAITH

It's almost impossible to discuss the nature of faith without turning to Hebrews 11. Here faith is both defined and illustrated in powerful statements that have become a part of the church's vocabulary and memory.

The author of Hebrews 11 was writing to a community of Jewish Christians who evidently were undergoing a trial so severe that they were being tempted to turn back from following Christ. In Hebrews 11:1, we are told that faith is "the assurance of things hoped for, the conviction of things not seen." Faith connects us with that which our senses cannot detect. Faith is a firm conviction about something we cannot see, hear, feel, taste, or touch, but which is nevertheless very real (see 2 Cor. 4:18; Heb. 11:3). Faith brings the invisible realm into spiritual view.

Faith is not wishing upon a star, crossing our fingers and telling ourselves to have faith in faith itself, or hoping something is going to happen.

Read Romans 4:18-21 and answer the following: Based on what could be physically perceived, how much hope should Abraham have had?

_____

In the margin, record phrases from this passage that describe Abraham's faith.

On what was Abraham's faith based?

_____

Biblical faith is a settled confidence in the person and the promises of God as revealed in His Word. Faith trusts in the integrity of God because it believes God has told the truth about unseen realities.

The Bible says, "We walk by faith, not by sight" (2 Cor. 5:7). Paul was even more specific about the contrast between faith and sight in Romans 8: "For in hope we have been saved, but hope that is seen is not hope; for who hopes for what he already sees? But if we hope for what we do not see, with perseverance we wait eagerly for it" (vv. 24-25).

The reason many of us as Christians are not growing and seeing more of the life of Christ being expressed through us is that our faith does not reach beyond our sight. The Bible says it is impossible to please God without faith (see Heb. 11:6). When we are not pleasing God because of our refusal to trust in Him, we won't see Him at work in our lives. When we can see it, we don't feel the need to trust God for it. And since we can't see very far, living by sight keeps us living small.

Biblical faith has substance because God has substance. The more you know about the character and promises of God, the more substance your faith will have. And the more faith you have, the more of God you will experience and the more growth will take place in your life.

Faith establishes what we think about God, and I'm afraid that many of us as His children act like we have more confidence in ourselves than we do in Him. The faith heroes in Hebrews 11 were people who acted on what

"The more you know about the character and promises of God, the more substance your faith will have."
—Tony Evans

they said they believed. Noah believed and got out his hammer and saw to build the ark. Abraham believed and put a "for sale" sign in his front yard in Ur. Moses believed and left Pharaoh's palace to identify with Hebrew slaves. Don't say you have faith and sit where you are.

Someone could argue that people like Noah, Abraham, and Moses had it easier than we do because God spoke to them directly. God did speak to them, but that didn't make their obedience any easier. We actually have an advantage over earlier saints because we have God's completed Word. He speaks to us as surely as He spoke to the patriarchs. But we still have to experience the turbulence of life.

Based on what can be physically perceived in your present circumstance, how much hope should you

have?_____

What words or phrases describe your faith?

_____

On what are you basing your faith?

_____

day *Five*

Faith

THE MECHANISM OF FAITH

Along with faith's meaning, it is also important to understand the way faith works and what it does. This is not to suggest that faith is a mechanical process, but that the Bible gives us clues into how faith operates in our lives.

One of these clues on faith is sort of buried in the middle of Ephesians 3:14-21 in which Paul prayed that his readers would gain spiritual insight.

Read Ephesians 3:14,16-17a printed in the margin. Underline why Paul prayed believers would experience the Holy Spirit's power in their inner being.

"I bow my knees before the Father ... that He would grant you, according to the riches of His glory, to be strengthened with power through His Spirit in the inner man, so that Christ may dwell in your hearts through faith" (Eph. 3:14,16-17a).

113

The word *dwell* here means more than just to move in and take up residence. It means to be at home, to make yourself comfortable, to spread out and have the run of the house. Paul was praying that the Ephesian believers would allow Christ to have complete control of their lives so that He could make Himself at home in their hearts and produce growth and spiritual fruit through the power of the Holy Spirit.

Faith is not only the mechanism by which Christ comes into our lives. It is also the mechanism or the means by which we give Him freedom to enter every room and do whatever He wants to do there, including throwing out the old stuff and redecorating.

If you want to grow as a Christian, Christ needs to be at home in your heart. And you make Him at home by faith. When you give Him the keys to the home of your heart, He "decorates" it with love, joy, peace, and the other fruit of the Holy Spirit. Paul went on in Ephesians 3 to pray that we might "be able to comprehend with all the saints what is the breadth and length and height and depth, and to know the love of Christ, which surpasses knowledge, that you may be filled up to all the fullness of God" (vv. 18-19). This is the kind of spiritual growth you can anticipate when you make Christ at home.

THE MEASUREMENT OF FAITH

Since faith is an action, are there ways we can tell when we are growing in the grace and knowledge of Jesus Christ? In James 2 we find a powerful and very practical yardstick for measuring the size of our faith. James began the discussion by posing this question: "What use is it, my brethren, if someone says he has faith but he has no works? Can that faith save him?" (Jas. 2:14).

James is not talking about faith in terms of how we are saved and get to heaven, but in terms of how we live here on earth. That's why he gives the illustration of the brother or sister in need who is turned away by a fellow believer empty-handed with this hollow blessing: "Go in peace, be warmed and be filled" (v. 16). James then makes the poignant statement, "Even so faith, if it has no works, is dead, being by itself" (v. 17).

A lot of Christians are wasting their time going to church because they hear the Word with their ears, but they are not doing anything about what they are hearing. True faith will produce works because it is an action. If you want to measure your faith, look at the response it is producing or failing to produce.

"What use is it, my brethren, if someone says he has faith but he has no works? Can that faith save him? If a brother or sister is without clothing and in need of daily food, and one of you says to them, 'Go in peace, be warmed and be filled,' and yet you do not give them what is necessary for their body, what use is that? Even so faith, if it has no works, is dead, being by itself" (Jas. 2:14-17).

As James was making his point that genuine faith produces actions that can be seen and measured, he turned to an incident in the life of Abraham (see Jas. 2:21-23). This was the offering of Isaac, probably the single greatest act of faith that any human being has ever been asked to perform. You can review the story in Genesis 22. James asked, "Was not Abraham our father justified by works when he offered up Isaac his son on the altar?" (v. 21).

Abraham had believed God and been justified, but God still wanted to see Abraham demonstrate his faith. After the Lord stopped Abraham from killing Isaac, he said, "Now I know that you fear God" (Gen. 22:12). Didn't God already know Abraham's faith was real? Of course He did. But Abraham needed to know it too, and the best way to learn that was to undergo a trial of faith. God wants to see if we will trust Him, and He wants us to see if we will trust Him when what He tells us to do seems to make no sense.

"Was not Abraham our father justified by works when he offered up Isaac his son on the altar? You see that faith was working with his works, and as a result of the works, faith was perfected; and the Scripture was fulfilled which says, 'AND ABRAHAM BELIEVED GOD, AND IT WAS RECKONED TO HIM AS RIGHTEOUSNESS,' and he was called the friend of God" (Jas. 2:21-23).

How do you think Abraham grew spiritually after seeing God spare Isaac?

_____

_____

Describe how you have grown spiritually by trusting God even when His ways didn't seem to make sense.

_____

_____

God also tries our faith so we can have the experience of walking with Him through the trial and proving Him faithful. It's one thing to say we trust God, but it's another thing to be able to say, "I know God is real because I trusted Him in the fire and He brought me through." God loves to see us trust Him over our friends, our feelings, and our logic.

God's desire is to take you higher, but He can only do that if He can fill you with Himself. And He can't fill you with Himself until you trust Him. And you aren't really trusting Him until you are willing to walk by faith, instead of just talk by faith. Is there an area where you need to trust God right now? Do by faith what He has asked you to do, and watch your spiritual life blossom.

To the Leader:

This lesson offers many opportunities to demonstrate with the sugar, funnel, and bowl what blocks the flow of God's grace and prevents spiritual growth. If you choose to do these visual demonstrations, it would be a good idea to practice a few times to make sure you "get it" before you demonstrate it for the class!

Before the Session

Gather a five-pound bag of sugar with scoop, a medium glass bowl, and a funnel to use during the session.

During the Session

1. Ask: *What bad habits do parents warn will stunt growth? What really stunts growth?* OR Display the sugar and explain it represents the grace God wants to pour into believers' lives so they can grow. Hold the funnel over the bowl with your fingers near the bottom opening, pour some sugar into the funnel and after some has poured through, block the funnel with your fingertip. Explain that unfortunately many Christians are not growing because something is blocking the flow of grace. FOR EITHER OPTION Share that you will look at what is blocking God's "spiritual growth hormone" of grace in believers and stunting spiritual growth. More importantly, you will be challenged to remove those hindrances so you can experience maximum spiritual growth (if you used the second option remove your finger as you make that final statement and let more sugar flow through).

2. Ask the class to share the biggest hindrance to spiritual growth. Ask them to share the complete contrast declared in 1 John 1:5-6. Ask: *What do your eyes do when you step into the dark? What happens when you allow sin to remain in your life?* [We adjust to it until it doesn't look so bad.] Ask someone to read the quotation in the margin of Day 1 (p. 106). Inquire: *What won't flow in your life if God is absent?* [His grace and power.] *What will that do to your spiritual growth?* Discuss the final activity of Day 1.

3. Ask what two choices we have when we become aware of sin in our lives. Discuss the first activity of Day 2. Cover the bottom of the funnel and pour more sugar into the funnel. Unblock the funnel and explain that confession removes sin so grace can flow and we can grow. Lead the class to explore how Isaiah's experience in Isaiah 6:1-7 illustrates the principles you've learned so far about sin, grace, and growth.

4. Draw attention to the bag of sugar and the small bowl. Ask which will run out first—the sugar or room in the bowl. Explain that the spiritual growth of many Christians is limited because their understanding of and response to God's grace is too small. Lead the class to define *grace*. Discuss the final activity of Day 2 (p. 108). Ask a volunteer to read Ephesians 2:4-7. Write "But God …" on the board. Ask: W*hat is the beauty of those two words? What has God's grace done for us? Can we ever run out of God's grace?* Ask participants to share from 2 Corinthians 12:9 what Paul learned about God's grace. Discuss: *When do we have trouble believing His grace is enough? What do we need to realize about God's grace when problems come?* Invite someone to read Ephesians 2:8-10. Ask how a believer should respond to God's grace (p. 110). Ask participants to read 1 Corinthians 15:9-10. Ask: *What did grace do in Paul's life? What was his response to this grace? Did he work for God out of obligation or because of his relationship with Christ? What's the difference?*

5. Ask what is partnered with grace in Ephesians 2:8. Organize the class into two groups. Instruct one group to use principles from Romans 8:24-25; 2 Corinthians 4:18; Hebrews 11:1-3; and the material in Day 4 to answer, "What is faith?" Instruct the second group to use the same texts to answer, "What is not faith?" Allow groups to share their answers. Ask: *Why is faith that goes beyond sight essential to spiritual growth? How can we add more substance to our faith?*

6. Discuss the first activity of Day 5 (p. 113). Explain the meaning of *dwell*. Ask participants to name TV home improvement/makeover programs. Ask: *How much faith do these homeowners place in others when they give them their house key? Do you place that much faith in Christ to renovate your life?* Ask how we can tell we are growing in Christ. Read James 2:14-17.

7. Read Ephesians 3:17b-19. Pour sugar through the funnel until the bowl is filled. Explain that this is the kind of spiritual growth we can experience when we confess our sins, live in grace by faith, and make Christ completely at home in our hearts. Read Ephesians 3:14-20 as your closing prayer.

The Holy Spirit, Scripture, and Prayer

day**O**ne

The Holy Spirit:
The Enabler for Spiritual Growth

The Holy Spirit is God's supernatural gift to make experiential, alive, and real the new beings we have become. The Spirit is the heart and soul of a growing, flourishing Christian life, and if we don't get plugged into Him, we will continue to stagnate and remain stunted in our spiritual development. However, once we are plugged in to the Spirit, we will experience the supernatural wonder of a life in which the power of God's grace flows.

GOD'S GIFT OF THE HOLY SPIRIT

The indwelling Holy Spirit is God's great gift to us. Unfortunately, many believers today know who the Holy Spirit is, but they don't know what He does or why He is important.

As believers living on this side of the cross, we are accustomed to Jesus' physical absence and the Holy Spirit's invisible presence because we never knew what it was like for Jesus to walk among us. But His disciples had experienced that, so when on the night before His crucifixion Jesus announced His departure and the Holy Spirit's coming, it created a huge crisis.

Jesus announced, "Where I am going, you cannot come" (John 13:33). How were the disciples going to make it on earth if Jesus went back to heaven? Jesus knew the disciples were deeply troubled, so He answered their questions with this promise: "I will ask the Father, and He will give you another Helper, that He may be with you forever" (John 14:16).

Read the following verses and note what you learn about the Holy Spirit.

118

John 14:17: _____

John 14:26: _____

God was not sending His people a cheap substitute for Jesus but someone just like Him—meaning of the same essence and character as Christ. The Holy Spirit shares the same divine essence as Jesus.

If you know Christ as your Savior, the Holy Spirit lives within you at the very depths of your inner being. Christians in whom the Holy Spirit is allowed to flow freely will grow and flourish in ways they never thought possible. Jesus said, "Apart from Me you can do nothing" (John 15:5). The Spirit is the divine enabler for spiritual growth.

> "Christians in whom the Holy Spirit is allowed to flow freely will grow and flourish in ways they never thought possible." —Tony Evans

OUR NEED OF THE SPIRIT'S FILLING

Even though every Christian possesses the Holy Spirit, it is possible to experience very little of His power and influence in our day-to-day lives. The issue is not how much of the Spirit we have but how much He has of us.

According to Ephesians 5:18, what are believers commanded to do?

_____

The more consistently you and I are filled with the Holy Spirit, the faster we will grow in our faith. But the less filled we are, the slower will be our growth. The basic meaning of the command "be filled with" is to be controlled by. When we are filled in the New Testament sense, it means somebody or something else has taken over the command center of our lives and is calling the shots. We are no longer in control.

The purpose of the Holy Spirit's filling is that He might control our lives. This command is in a form in the original language that means "keep on being filled" as a continuous process. The filling must be constantly and continuously renewed. That's why rather than spending our time, energy, and effort trying to change, we need to spend our time getting filled.

THE PROCESS OF BEING FILLED

If being filled with the Spirit is key to growth and power as Christians, we need to ask how a person experiences the Spirit's filling. This question is answered in Ephesians 5:19-21. Read it in the margin. Paul's concern here is

> "Speaking to one another in psalms and hymns and spiritual songs, singing and making melody with your heart to the Lord; always giving thanks for all things in the name of our Lord Jesus Christ to God, even the Father; and be subject to one another in the fear of Christ" (Eph. 5:19–21).

119

to tell us how to be filled and keep being filled with the Holy Spirit. The Holy Spirit's filling is made real when we make worship our lifestyle.

Remember times when you left church on Sunday spiritually full? You poured out your heart to God and you were filled with a sense of His holy presence. The way you learn to live a Spirit-filled life is to learn to do Monday through Saturday what you did on Sunday.

You left church on Sunday full of the Spirit because you were in God's presence with God's people, communing with Him. But when you go out on Monday and start jostling with people in a sin-soaked, sick world, your experience of the Spirit's filling can get depleted in a hurry.

We need to learn to draw on the Spirit's filling as a day-by-day way of life. We do this as we commune with God by making decisions in accordance with His Word, with a song in our hearts, a spirit of thanksgiving to Him, and an attitude of humble submission toward other believers.

Grade yourself (A,B,C,D,F) in the following areas:
___ making decisions based on God's Word
___ keeping a song of praise in my heart
___ thanking God for all things
___ having a humble, submissive attitude toward others

day Two

The Holy Spirit and Scripture

THE IMPORTANCE OF WALKING BY THE SPIRIT

"Walk by the Spirit, and you will not carry out the desire of the flesh. For the flesh sets its desire against the Spirit, and the Spirit against the flesh; for these are in opposition to one another, so that you may not do the things that you please" (Gal. 5:16-17).

The Bible tells us again and again that God and the flesh will never get along because they are diametrically opposed to each other. The struggle comes because we are still in our sinful flesh, and we will be until Christ returns and gives us new bodies. That's why Paul had to exhort us to walk by the Spirit so we won't fulfill the flesh's wrong desires.

It's not that if we are filled with the Holy Spirit we will never have the desires of the flesh. It's that when the Spirit is in control, the flesh won't have the last word in our lives.

WALKING BY THE SPIRIT IS A DAILY PROCESS

Walking has three components we don't usually think about, but it is helpful to consider them when we're talking about our spiritual walk.

First of all, walking involves a destination. When you walk, you're going somewhere. Walking by the Spirit involves a destination too, because He is ever and always moving us toward a destination, which is God's glory.

Second, walking requires dedication. Walking must continue if we are to make progress. It's like the Holy Spirit's filling, which must be renewed regularly. It must be ongoing.

A third component of walking is dependence. You have to put your weight down on one leg and then another to walk. Or if your legs aren't working properly, you have to depend on something or someone else to get you where you're going. Either way demands dependence. When you recognize your dependence, you are ready to learn what it means to walk by the Spirit. When you learn to depend on God, you get stronger and not weaker.

There is no restriction on how fast you can grow or how far you can go in the Christian life. The Holy Spirit will take you as far and as fast as you are willing to depend on Him.

Read Galatians 5:22-23. Describe the spiritual growth that occurs when believers walk by the Spirit.

> "There is no restriction on how fast you can grow or how far you can go in the Christian life. The Holy Spirit will take you as far and as fast as you are willing to depend on Him."
> —Tony Evans

_____

_____

SCRIPTURE: THE FOOD OF SPIRITUAL GROWTH

Jesus Christ explicitly stated the connection between spiritual health and the Word of God when He said, "Man shall not live on bread alone, but on every word that proceeds out of the mouth of God" (Matt. 4:4).

The Bible is the inspired, inerrant revelation of God. Its purpose is not just to give us information for our heads but food for the new nature to feed upon so that spiritual growth can be maximized.

THE IMPORTANCE OF SPIRITUAL MILK

Peter certainly knew what picture to grab on to when he wanted to urge believers to long for God's Word. "Like newborn babies, long for the pure milk of the word, so that by it you may grow in respect to salvation" (1 Pet. 2:2). What milk is to a baby's body, the Word of God is to the soul. It is the food that fuels healthy spiritual growth.

Peter referred to the Word as "pure" milk, the real stuff. Too many Christians are undernourished because they feed on substitutes. God warns us not to accept anything but the authentic, undiluted truth of Scripture. This truth of Scripture is diluted when it goes unaddressed in our lives. The truth of God can't nourish us because of the contamination it must pass through.

Other believers have forgotten the importance of a regular feeding schedule for their spiritual growth. We can't stuff ourselves on Sunday and live off that until the next Sunday. But that's what many Christians try to do spiritually, and then they wonder why they are not growing.

Believers who aren't regularly feeding on God's Word are malnourished. It's not enough just to be under the teaching of the Bible weekly in church. We also need to be in the Word daily for ourselves.

"They are not meaningless words to you but they are your life" (Deut. 32:47, HCSB).

"I have treasured the words of His mouth more than my daily food" (Job 23:12, HCSB).

"I rise before dawn and cry out for help; I put my hope in your word" (Ps. 119:147, HCSB).

Read the Scriptures printed in the margin. List actions and attitudes in your life that demonstrate God's Word is:

your life: _____

your treasure: _____

your hope: _____

day Three

Scripture

SAVORING THE MEAT OF THE WORD

The comparison to baby's milk lets us know that it is the basics of the Christian faith. Babies don't begin with solid food. They need milk until their digestive systems are ready for something more. Milk is crucial for a new Christian to feed on, but it is not the whole meal.

The Bible makes a distinction between the milk and the meat, or solid food, of God's Word in terms of content and level of difficulty. God also tells us what this more advanced diet should be producing within us.

Read Hebrews 5:12–6:2. Use the chart below to contrast spiritual milk and solid food.

Milk	Solid Food

Solid food refers to the spiritual understanding and application to the experience of truth operating in the believer's life. That's why Hebrews 5:14 makes this crucial statement: "Solid food is for the mature, who because of practice have their senses trained to discern good and evil." Mature believers have the capacity to perceive the spiritual nature of things and then function and make choices based on this spiritual insight. The more consistently you connect doctrine (milk) with spiritual discernment and life application (meat), the more mature you are. With maturity comes the increased capacity to experientially perceive things from a divine perspective.

When it comes to God's Word, meat-eaters are those who can digest the truth so that they have a heavenly rather than an earthly response to the issues they face in life. They can turn that nourishment into solid spiritual growth.

The question isn't whether milk or solid food is more important to our growth and development. Both are important at the proper time, even though they are different. The milk stage of our growth has more to do with the doctrinal truth we take in, the basics that we need to have to lay a good foundation for later growth. But once people have fed on the milk of God's Word, we want them to go on. This was the hope the writer of Hebrews expressed for his readers: "Leaving the elementary teaching about the Christ, let us press on to maturity" (6:1).

GRADUATING FROM MILK TO MEAT

The way we grow from milk to meat is by applying the truths of God's Word to cultivate our relationship with Jesus Christ. This intimacy when applied, especially during times of trials, produces great growth. There is a strong link between food and relationship both in the natural and the spiritual world.

A long-distance love relationship doesn't depend on sight but on the impact of words. When two people are relating this way, they are going beyond the mere passing of information to the meaning behind the information. Too many Christians view the Bible as a library of information to be studied and learned. When you feed on God's Word with the purpose in mind of getting to know the person behind the page, it changes everything.

To develop spiritual maturity requires that you read God's Word so you know what it says, study the Word so you know what it means, memorize the Word so you can use it when you need it, and take every opportunity to hear the Word of God proclaimed and taught so you can learn to live life and make decisions based on it. When you give this kind of serious attention to the Scriptures, spiritual growth is inevitable.

God's Word is good for you. If you're in good shape right now, it will be sweet honey to nourish your soul. If you have a messed-up heart, a confused mind, or damaged relationships, take the Word. It's good for what ails you.

If you will drink the pure milk of God's infallible Word and graduate to its solid food, you will discover that it's good for you because you will grow in grace and the knowledge of our Lord Jesus Christ. Then you will be able to say with the prophet Jeremiah, "Your words were found and I ate them, and Your words became for me a joy and the delight of my heart; for I have been called by Your name, O LORD God of hosts" (15:16).

Check the statement that best describes your appetite for the deeper truths of God's Word:
- ❏ I've lost my appetite.
- ❏ I'm starving for it.
- ❏ I'd like just a taste.
- ❏ I feast on it daily.

Prayer: The Access of Spiritual Growth

Prayer is the primary means by which we relate to God. Prayer is a dialogue between two people who are intimately related, not a monologue in which one person does all the talking and the other does all the listening. Prayer is part of a relationship with God to be cultivated.

God has made us in such a way that the power of the Holy Spirit flows along the wires of prayer, which makes prayer absolutely vital and central to all of life—including our spiritual growth. Prayer is so important that the Bible tells us, "Pray without ceasing" (1 Thess. 5:17).

PRAYER GIVES US ACCESS TO HEAVEN

Heaven is where our Father lives, and prayer is the means by which we relate to and communicate with Him. The goal in prayer is to enter our Father's presence the way a child comes to a father he knows loves him.

Prayer as relational communication with God is a wonderful concept, but if we are honest, we would also have to admit that sometimes the spiritual world feels like a foreign land to us.

The Holy Spirit is the perfect Teacher for that task. One of His jobs is to teach us the language of prayer and guide us in learning how to pray.

What comforting truth about prayer do you discover in Romans 8:26?

_____

The Holy Spirit understands prayers that we can't express adequately and makes sense of thoughts we don't understand ourselves, because He knows the language of prayer and can interpret it to us.

This spiritual communication with God helps turn what was a strange and foreign land into a wonderful new world. When we pray, we are transported to another world that is completely different from our everyday world. Prayer positions us to hear from God so that our new spiritual nature is ready to be spoken to by the Holy Spirit. Then we are ready to hear God's voice applying His Word to our specific needs and circumstances.

Jesus had a lot to say about prayer during His ministry on earth. One of those occasions was during the Sermon on the Mount, when Jesus taught some very crucial principles of prayer.

Use the chart to contrast the do's and don'ts of prayer according to Matthew 6:5-8.

Do	Don't

Jesus said prayer was not to be a public demonstration of our piety, nor was it a matter of saying all the right words in the right order. The intimate nature of our communication with God is illustrated by going into a closet and closing the door behind us to pray. Why shut the door? Because it's just you and your Father in a family discussion.

Jesus said you don't need to worry about getting all the words right because "your Father knows what you need before you ask Him" (Matt. 6:8). God still wants you to ask, but because He is your Father He is listening to your heart as much as or more than your words.

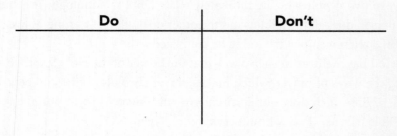

day Five

Four Great Truths About Prayer

There are four great truths in Hebrews 4:14-16 (printed in the margin) that can turn anyone's prayer life from dormant to dynamic.

WE HAVE AN INTERCESSOR IN THE PERSON OF CHRIST
The writer of Hebrews tells us the most important fact about our High Priest, which is His identity. "Jesus the Son of God" is a great title for our Lord,

"Since we have a great high priest who has passed through the heavens, Jesus the Son of God, let us hold fast our confession. For we do not have a high priest who cannot sympathize with our weaknesses, but One who has been tempted in all things as we are, yet without sin. Therefore let us draw near with confidence to the throne of grace, so that we may receive mercy and find grace to help in time of need" (Heb. 4:14-16).

indicating both His humanity as Jesus and His deity as God's Son. Jesus is unique in eternity and in history because He is the God-man. As man, He can feel what we feel, and as God, He can fix what makes us feel that way.

Jesus can understand what you are going through when you cry out to Him, and He has the power of God to act. A priest represents the people to God and God to the people, and we have a High Priest who understands both sides perfectly.

WE HAVE ACCESS TO GOD THROUGH THE POSITION OF CHRIST

Jesus is also unique in the position He holds. He has "passed through the heavens" (v. 14). The Bible says Jesus passed through the heavens and entered the holy place in the heavenly temple to offer one sacrifice forever for our sins (see Heb. 9:24-26).

When we pray in the power of the Holy Spirit, Jesus Christ as our Priest and Intercessor makes sure our prayer gets to the proper location, the presence of God, where our needs and concerns can be addressed. Because Jesus, the Son of God, is related to the Father, He can bypass all the stuff that blocks you and me. That's why when we pray, we pray in Jesus' name.

> **Read the Scriptures below. Draw a line from the reference to the action Jesus takes on your behalf.**

1 Timothy 2:5   **Speaks to the Father as my advocate**

Hebrews 7:25   **Mediates between me and God**

1 John 2:1   **Intercedes for me.**

WE HAVE A SYMPATHETIC PRIEST THROUGH THE PASSION OF CHRIST

Jesus sympathizes with our weaknesses because He has experienced every temptation we will ever face, except that Jesus never sinned. Why do we need a High Priest who knows what it's like to be tempted, to be tired and hungry and sad and all the other feelings and emotions we feel? So He can represent and interpret these feelings to God the Father.

Although God the Father has full knowledge of everything, He does not have full experience of everything. For example, God the Father has never been tempted to sin the way we are tempted.

God the Father wanted to relate to you and me on the feeling level. So He sent His precious Son to earth and gave Him a human body and emotions like ours so the Son could live among us and feel everything we feel. Because Jesus did that, He can interpret our feelings and our needs to His Father.

You may say, "Yes, but Jesus was without sin, so He can't really feel my sin the way I feel it." Oh, but He can. In fact, because of His purity He actually feels the pain of sin even more. Jesus' separateness from sin does not diminish His ability to sympathize with us.

"Jesus' separateness from sin does not diminish His ability to sympathize with us."
—Tony Evans

WE CAN DRAW NEAR THROUGH THE PROVISION OF CHRIST

Do you understand what it means to be invited to draw near to God, to go right up to His throne? God's people couldn't do this in the Old Testament days. Only the high priest could draw near once a year. Everybody else had to wait to see if God would accept the high priest's sacrifice and cover their sins for another year. But Jesus has satisfied the demands of God so that we can have direct access to Him.

God says you have been duly authorized to enter His throne room by virtue of your connection with Christ. This is not the throne where you find judgment but mercy and grace. This is where all the power and authority you will ever need reside. This is where God gives His sons and daughters what we could never give ourselves. All of this has been provided to you by Jesus Christ.

God gives us what we don't deserve and could never earn from a throne that never runs low on its provision—and it is all tied to our drawing near in prayer. God has all the grace we need to help us, but we have to go before the throne to ask for this grace. When we tap into the power of prayer, we will start to grow in leaps and bounds as our new nature grows stronger in the spiritual environment it was made to inhabit.

Draw near to Him. He will meet you where you are and take you before the throne that dispenses grace. No matter what may be happening in your life, Jesus, the Son of God, stands ready to lead you directly into His Father's presence, where there is grace unlimited to meet your needs.

A prayerless Christian is a graceless Christian.
Do you ❑ agree OR ❑ disagree? Explain your answer in the margin.

A prayerless Christian is a Christian who isn't growing.
Do you ❑ agree OR ❑ disagree? Explain your answer in the margin.

To the Leader:

Every time you drink, eat, or are aware of drawing a breath this week ask the Spirit to empower you to convey these life essentials to your class in new and powerful ways.

During the Session

1. Ask: *What is absolutely essential for life?* OR Organize the class into several small groups and instruct them to list the supplies they would take on a wilderness survival trip. Allow groups to share and explain why they chose the supplies they did. FOR EITHER OPTION Explain that the essentials for life are water, food, and air. Today you will see those are also the life essentials for Christian life and growth.

2. Invite a volunteer to read John 7:37-39. Ask participants to identify the water that flows into and out of every believer. Discuss the first activity of Day 1 (pp. 118-19). Ask: *If every Christian has the Holy Spirit, why are many not experiencing His power?* Discuss the second activity of Day 1. Ask why participants think Paul used drunkenness as an analogy for being Spirit-filled. Explain that just as alcohol negatively controls how a person acts, thinks, and speaks, so the Holy Spirit must be allowed to positively control believers' lives. Invite someone to read Ephesians 5:19-21. Ask how we can be filled with the Spirit. Ask if participants can recall worship services when the Spirit's presence was really strong. Invite them to share what occurred in those times of worship. Ask: *Can you drink your week's supply of water in a couple of hours so you won't have to worry about it the rest of the week? Why? Can we get filled with the Spirit for a couple of hours on Sunday and that be enough for the week? Why? How can we be filled with the Spirit daily?* Encourage participants to silently consider the evaluation activity at the conclusion of Day 1 (p. 120). Request that someone read Galatians 5:16-17. Explain that the issue in Ephesians 5 is who is in control, while in Galatians 5 the issue is who will win the battle. Inquire: *What is the battle? How is the battle won?* Use the material in Day 2 to explore what it means to walk by the Spirit.

3. Explain that in addition to needing the water of the Holy Spirit, our new nature also needs food. Ask participants to identify the food of spiritual growth. Read Matthew 4:4. Ask what food a new baby needs to grow properly. Read 1 Peter 2:2. Guide the class to describe how a newborn

"longs" for milk. Ask: *What percentage of Christians would you say are malnourished? Why?* Encourage them to use the material in Day 2 to form their responses. Read the passages in the margin of Day 2 (p. 122). Guide participants to describe the actions and attitudes of believers for whom God's Word is their life, treasure, and hope.

4. Ask participants how they would respond if they saw a grown man sucking on a bottle. Remind them that just as people need to grow up in their eating habits, so should believers. Discuss the first activity of Day 3. Explain that milk is the important basics of the Christian faith. Inquire: *What basics of education did you learn in elementary school? Was that enough? Why? What did you need to do with those basics? What do we need to do with the basics of Christian doctrine?* Request that participants read 1 Corinthians 3:1-3 and share why some Christians are still sucking a bottle instead of eating solid food. Discuss how Christians can graduate from milk to meat. Share: *A healthy growing diet is balanced and includes vegetables along with steaks and sweets. We are to eat all of God's Word because it's always good for you even if it doesn't always taste good!*

5. Ask: *Does anyone have to tell you when to breathe? Why?* Read 1 Thessalonians 5:17. Explain that just as breathing is the link to our earthly existence, prayer is the link to our heavenly existence and should come as unconsciously as drawing each breath. Ask participants if prayer is as easy as breathing to them and why. Discuss the first activity of Day 4 (p. 125). Ask someone to read Hebrews 4:14-16. Discuss how the truths in this passage can turn someone's prayer life from dormant to dynamic. Request someone read Job 9:32-35. Ask participants how they would have responded to Job's complaint. Use the final activity of Day 4 to discuss the do's and don'ts of prayer. Discuss the final activity of Day 5. Close in prayer.

The Church and Giving

day One

The Church: The Context of Spiritual Growth

God designed Christians to be born, protected, and raised in the context of a community known as the church. The Bible says that our enemy, the Devil, "prowls around like a roaring lion, seeking someone to devour" (1 Pet. 5:8). One of the easiest people to devour is the Christian who is no longer functioning within the nurturing context of the church.

God never meant for us grow and develop spiritually in isolation from other believers. Spiritual growth is a group project. Christians grow best in a healthy family context where they are surrounded by spiritual fathers, mothers, brothers, and sisters to help them.

The Bible uses a number of terms to illustrate this community or corporate aspect of the church. One of these terms is *family*. If you are a Christian, you are a part of God's family. But a lot of God's children are trying to live as if they don't need anyone else. Believers who are not functioning as part of a local church are outside of God's will, which means they are undermining their own spiritual development.

Some people will tell you they believe in the church as a concept, but they aren't interested in plugging in to a local body of believers. Christianity doesn't work that way. Jesus Christ is so committed to this family called the church that He died and rose again to redeem us, and He has invested all of heaven's resources in the church's life.

Read Ephesians 5:25-27,29-30. What actions does Jesus take on behalf of His church?

_____

_____

What is Christ's goal for His church?

_____

THE CHURCH'S VITAL ROLE IN SPIRITUAL GROWTH

The church is not just a classroom for spiritual instruction but a living and growing organism to enhance our spiritual development. No portion of Scripture teaches the importance of the church to the spiritual development of its members better than the Book of Ephesians. Paul made a foundational statement about the church in Ephesians 2:19-22.

As you read that passage printed in the margin, underline the italicized words.

The words I've emphasized tell us that we are part of something bigger than any one of us. I see no mention here of individual growth apart from the church. The pronouns are all plural. We grow as we are connected because it is the church together that experiences the unique presence of God.

There are some things God will do for you just because you are one of His children. Every believer is saved, sealed with the Holy Spirit, and assured of heaven. Every believer has been baptized by the Holy Spirit into the body of Christ (see 1 Cor. 12:13). But there are many other things God will only do for you when you are a functioning member of His body. Spiritual growth is one of those blessings that can only be fully realized in the context of the church.

Read Hebrews 10:24-25 and fill in the blanks.

Believers are commanded to _____

in order that _____ .

There are times when we need to go into the privacy of our prayer closet. But there are other things we can only experience in the ambiance of God's people gathered in the church. The church is the corporate dwelling place of the Holy Spirit. When people who are individually indwelled by the Spirit come together for worship, praise, instruction, encouragement, and service, the Holy Spirit shows up in a powerful way, and we grow as we experience His presence.

"You are no longer strangers and aliens, but you are _fellow citizens_ with the saints, and are of God's _household_, having been built on the foundation of the apostles and prophets, Christ Jesus Himself being the corner stone, in whom the whole _building_, being fitted together, is growing into a holy temple in the Lord, in whom you also are being _built together_ into a dwelling of God in the Spirit" (Eph. 2:19-22, emphasis added).

"Spiritual growth is one of those blessings that can only be fully realized in the context of the church." —Tony Evans

Jesus Christ went from the cross to the depths of hell to bring the church into being, and we cannot ignore what it cost Him to purchase His body, the church. The world and circumstances may beat us up all week and make us feel like losers, but when we gather with other members of Christ's body, we are reminded that we are on the winning side.

day Two

The Church as a Body

ATTACHMENT BEFORE GROWTH

The church as a concept may be ethereal and hard to grasp because our connection to other believers is invisible. But we can get hold of the concept of a body, because we all have one and we can see how it works. The human body is not an inanimate object but a living, growing, changing organism. The parts of our bodies have to stay connected to the body in order to function and grow. Many of us are stymied in our spiritual growth because we have cut ourselves off from the body.

Nothing will stimulate spiritual growth faster than when we experience the love of God's people, join other believers in serving the Lord, and draw on Christ and each other for regular encouragement.

The church provides the environment that stimulates our spiritual growth and development. Life has a way of deflating and discouraging us, and we need a place where we can be built up.

If you said to someone, "Would you like to come to a place where you will be loved, nurtured, encouraged, ministered to, and treasured as a valuable person?" most people would take you up on the deal. That's the way the church is supposed to treat its members, but don't miss something important here. I'm afraid the church has too many people who only want to feed and grow and give nothing back.

Read 1 Corinthians 12:14-26. What does God expect from every member of His church body?

_____

Spiritual growth is mutual, although there are times when a person needs to be ministered to and grow before he or she can help others grow.

WHAT WE NEED TO GROW

If you want to know where our spiritual growth is to lead, just look at Jesus Christ. This is a lifelong process we will never perfectly attain until we are face-to-face with Christ, but growth should be evident in our lives as we move from infancy to adulthood. One way you'll know you are growing is when your life takes on spiritual stability, as described in Ephesians 4:14. "We are no longer to be children, tossed here and there" by everything that blows in on the wind. That's how a lot of Christians are living. Every little struggle wipes them out. But God wants us to grow past this stage on our way to maturity in Christ.

"Speaking the truth in love, we are to grow up in all aspects into Him who is the head, even Christ" (Eph. 4:15).

As you read Ephesians 4:15 printed in the margin, underline two things that need to be present in our lives and supplied by the church if we are to grow up.

Truth is a fixed standard by which everything else is measured. The Holy Spirit's ministry in the church is key to the body's growth, but the Holy Spirit only works in the environment of truth. Jesus called Him "the Spirit of truth" (John 14:17). The Spirit's job is to reveal the truth of God's Word and confirm it in our hearts, and the church is the center for promoting, proclaiming, and protecting God's truth.

For truth to stimulate growth, it must be handled and applied with a spirit of love and concern for the people to whom it is being communicated. This explains why there is such a major emphasis in the Epistles on the "one another," or relational, aspect of the church's ministry. The New Testament Epistles were written either to local churches or to individuals who had oversight of local churches. What that says to us is that God works with us individually as we are part of His spiritual community called the church.

"From him the whole body, joined and held together by every supporting ligament, grows and builds itself up in love, as each part does its work" (Eph. 4:16, NIV).

According to Ephesians 4:16 (printed in the margin) is spiritual growth a ❑ solo act or ❑ group project?

The church grows when every individual part is doing its job and contributing to the whole. In the same way, the lack of growth by some members affects the entire body. Your individual part is critical to the whole, and when you are fulfilling your part, God will make sure you grow.

When believers are growing together in unity and love, a lot of problems are taken care of before they become big because the body is healing itself. A healthy body that is working the way it was designed to work will grow, and every member of that body will benefit.

When God put together the human body, He did it so that every part would be vital for the working of every other part. The church functions the same way. If you are not in a church where God's Word is being taught in an atmosphere of love, you need to find a place where the body is functioning as God intended. You need it for the contribution you make to the body, and you need it for your own growth in Christ.

> "A healthy body that is working the way it was designed to work will grow, and every member of that body will benefit." —Tony Evans

Giving: The Generosity of Spiritual Growth

Throughout the Gospels, Jesus turned to money more than to any other subject when He wanted to teach us about the Christian life and illustrate what it means to follow Him. And some of the highest praise the Apostle Paul had for the believers he ministered to was related to their giving.

A POWERFUL INDICATOR OF SPIRITUAL GROWTH

Our attitude toward giving is much like the lights on a car's dashboard. When an indicator light comes on, it's pointing to something that needs attention. When God turns on the indicator light of money and giving in our lives, it's not because He is hurting for cash. He is looking at something deep in the heart that we cannot afford to ignore because He wants to deal with it.

Today many Christians suffer from a disease we might call "cirrhosis of the giver." This is a debilitating spiritual malady that has been around since the earliest days of the church, first being clearly diagnosed around A.D. 34 in a couple named Ananias and Sapphira, who became greedy with God's gifts and suffered the consequences (see Acts 5:1-11).

The disease of shriveled giving continues to plague the family of God. I say that based on the most recent figures that show the average Christian in

America gives only 2.5 percent of his or her income to the kingdom of God. The percentage of the average Christian's giving to the Lord has actually dropped from what it was about 30 years ago, when the figure was closer to 2.8 percent. This is an indicator that something is wrong "under the hood" of the church in America. Our spiritual priorities are out of place.

To help us get those priorities in order, we need to spend some time in 2 Corinthians 8–9, two of the most important chapters in the Bible on the subject of money and giving. I want you to see the connection between your giving and your spiritual growth, which will be evident as Paul wrote to urge the Corinthians to finish the collection for a special gift they had promised to send to the saints in Jerusalem who were in deep financial need. To encourage the Corinthians in their giving, Paul brought up the example of the Macedonian believers.

Read 2 Corinthians 8:1-5. Circle the words that describe how the Macedonian churches gave.

Begrudgingly   **Joyfully**   **Generously**

Out of their poverty   **Out of their leftovers**

What empowered them to give this way?

Their wealth   **God's grace**   **Their easy lives**

The Macedonians couldn't wait to give because they understood that they belonged to the Lord and whatever they had was a gift of His grace.

Once you connect your giving with God's grace, you give out of the overflow of God's goodness. Despite their poverty and afflictions, the Macedonians were experiencing an "abundance of joy" (2 Cor. 8:2) in the Lord that showed up in their attitude toward giving. That's key to remember, because in the Bible giving is connected to our spiritual life, not merely to our money—and the more that connection is made, the more spiritual growth will occur.

Over and over the Bible connects our giving with the flow of God's grace to us. Paul linked giving with Christ's sacrifice on the cross, pointing out that even though Christ had the riches of heaven at His disposal, He left it all and impoverished Himself by dying for us (see 2 Cor. 8:9).

Understanding how gracious God is to us is important because many people give to Him from their leftovers. If they have anything left after

"Once you connect your giving with God's grace, you give out of the overflow of God's goodness." —Tony Evans

"You know the grace of our Lord Jesus Christ, that though He was rich, yet for your sake He became poor, so that you through His poverty might become rich" (2 Cor. 8:9).

they've paid the bills and done everything they wanted to do, they'll give. But we need to know that even if we give God a million dollars, if it's out of our leftovers, we have insulted Him.

Everything God created was meant to give. He created the sun to give light during the day, the moon and the stars during the night. He created flowers to give seeds. Even Adam and Eve taught their sons to give, because the Bible says that Abel gave of the first of his flock to God (see Gen. 4:4). God is a giver: "For God so loved the world, that He gave" (John 3:16).

Read 2 Corinthians 8:7. List the areas where God wants you to grow.

_____

_____

Place a check by the areas that need work.

day *Four*

Giving Tithes and Offerings

THE PRINCIPLES OF SOWING AND REAPING

"He who sows sparingly will also reap sparingly, and he who sows bountifully will also reap bountifully" (2 Cor. 9:6). A farmer must start with his seed, not his need, if he has any hope of reaping a harvest. This fact is critical to the ministry of giving, because most people approach it from a need standpoint. Their reasoning is "I can't give to the Lord because I need to pay these bills," or whatever the case may be.

This is precisely the point at which faith must kick in. A farmer who plants is counting on nature to back him up, because all his planting does is position the seed for growth. Without proper sunlight and rain, nothing is going to happen, which means a lot of faith goes into farming.

Giving is also an act of faith in our great God. When He tells us to sow bountifully so we can reap bountifully, our willingness or reluctance to do that says a lot about whether we hold God and His promises in high esteem.

Another self-evident principle of sowing and reaping is that we will reap what we sow. We can't get apples if we sow oranges. Our harvest will be of the same nature as our seed. This principle not only refers to our financial giving but to our attitudes as well. If you're looking for love, how much love are you sowing? If you expect to receive a helping hand when you are in need, how are you doing in planting the seed of kindness and help in other people's lives?

So often the person who is quick to judge others is the first to plead for mercy and understanding when he messes up. A farmer doesn't shake his head in amazement if he gets a crop of corn from corn seed. But so often we shake our heads and wonder why God isn't blessing us with a harvest, forgetting that we haven't sown the right seed in the first place.

Most people have the philosophy, "Get all you can, can all you get, and then sit on the can." It's easy for Christians to adopt this philosophy, but why would we want to do so when God has offered us something so much better?

Read 2 Corinthians 9:10-11. What does God promise to do if you give generously?

_____

_____

GOD'S EXPECTATIONS OF HIS PEOPLE

The Bible has two words to express what God expects of us: tithes and offerings. The *tithe* was prescribed in the Old Testament, but the *offering* was a voluntary donation above and beyond the tithe. It was given out of gratitude to God for His bounty and blessing, and it was a further expression of love for and trust in Him.

How serious is God about this matter of our honoring Him with our tithes and offerings? We find out in Malachi 3, where God, through the prophet, rebukes His people for their greed and neglect of Him.

When it came to the nation's giving, God had a question. "Will a man rob God?" (v. 8). The people of Malachi's day played dumb and asked, "How have we robbed You?" (v. 8). God answered in the same verse: "In tithes and offerings." That is, they were using the portion that belonged to God for their own ends.

Some Christians are wearing clothes, driving cars, and going on vacations with God's tithes and offerings. Some of us are living in homes we can only afford by robbing from God's portion to pay the note each month. But God says we are stealing from Him. God says if we are robbing Him of His tithes and offerings, we should not think we are being blessed or getting away with it.

Read Malachi 3:9-10 printed in the margin.

Robbing God of His tithes and offerings results in

_____

Trusting God through giving results in

_____

" 'You are cursed with a curse, for you are robbing Me, the whole nation of you! Bring the whole tithe into the storehouse, so that there may be food in My house, and test Me now in this,' says the LORD of hosts, 'if I will not open for you the windows of heaven and pour out for you a blessing until it over-flows' " (Mal. 3:9-10).

Don't wait until you've paid your taxes or the Christmas shopping is done. Bring your fears to the Lord and test Him by giving Him your tithes and offerings even when you don't see how you are going to make it. When you take that step of faith, God will open the windows of heaven, another way of saying He will pour out His blessings, which are now behind closed and locked windows.

We don't throw open our windows when we know a thief is roaming the neighborhood. Neither does God open the windows of heaven for those who ignore or abuse His grace. You can't grow spiritually and be a thief at the same time.

A blessing is more than having more stuff. I'd love to be able to tell you that if you start giving to God the way He prescribes, He'll give you a new house or car. I would love to tell you that if you give faithfully, all of your problems will disappear. I can't make that promise. But what I can tell you is that God will give you a blessing, the capacity to enjoy, benefit from, and grow through what God gives you. A blessing is the presence of God in the midst of whatever He has provided.

day *Five*

Giving and Our Attitude

The Importance of Our Attitude

God is more interested in the attitude of your heart in giving than He is in calculating percentages.

> **What attitude toward giving is commended in the following verses?**
>
> **2 Corinthians 8:11-12** _____
>
> **2 Corinthians 9:7** _____

If the only way we'll give is when someone twists our arm or makes us feel guilty, God says He would just as soon we forget it because He is unhappy with a grudging giver.

You and I can be joyful in our giving when we understand that the only reason we have anything to give in the first place is that God gave to us. Deuteronomy 8:18 says it is God who gives us the power to make wealth. When you understand that God is the source of everything, you won't have any trouble being cheerful as you give to Him. And the more you grow in grace, the more cheerful a giver you'll be.

Let's say you have become the kind of cheerful giver that the Bible says God loves. He is pleased with your giving and the attitude of heart behind it. You are so excited about the opportunity and privilege you have to show God how much you love Him and how grateful you are that you can't wait for the offering plate to come by. You do your giving with joy because you know that without God's goodness to you, you wouldn't have the opportunity to return to Him your tithes and offerings.

If this is your attitude, the next verse applies to you—and it happens to be the greatest verse on grace in the Bible.

> **Look up 2 Corinthians 9:8 in your Bible and write it in the margin, capitalizing the word *all* each time it appears.**

"You shall remember the LORD your God, for it is He who is giving you power to make wealth, that He may confirm His covenant which He swore to your fathers, as it is this day" (Deut. 8:18).

When God sees a cheerful giver, He opens the floodgates of His grace and lets it flow unhindered. We've learned that grace is everything God does for us that we cannot do for ourselves. We can't earn or add to God's grace, but we can restrict its flow by our sinful attitudes, which in this case is an unwillingness to give. God's grace flows freely in the context of cheerful giving.

And don't ever think that your giving will outstrip God's grace. God's grace is always bigger than your gift. Isn't that true about farming? A farmer plants a corn seed, but he doesn't reap one kernel or even one ear. He reaps an entire stalk of corn from that one little seed. And that stalk not only supplies him with food, but it also provides him with more seeds to plant so he can repeat the process. In other words, God's grace just keeps on coming.

Giving is a spiritual act and a key ingredient in our spiritual growth. Paul told the Corinthians to lay aside their gifts "on the first day of every week" (1 Cor. 16:2). That's Sunday, the Lord's Day. In other words, giving is part of our worship. It's to be systematic and should reflect His bounty to us. Giving has to become a way of life for us as believers, and we never have to worry that God is going to slip up or forget about us.

Jesus Christ deserves your gifts, but He doesn't want you to give just because of what it does for Him. The important thing is what it does for you in terms of your spiritual growth and blessing. The primary beneficiary is not the receiver but the giver who lays up eternal treasure in heaven with each gift. When you give generously from the heart, you store up eternal reward while simultaneously accelerating your spiritual growth on earth.

Read Matthew 6:21 printed in the margin. Why do you think giving leads to spiritual growth?

> "When God sees a cheerful giver, He opens the floodgates of His grace and lets it flow unhindered."
> —Tony Evans

> "Where your treasure is, there your heart will be also" (Matt. 6:21).

Are you afraid to test God in the area of giving and afraid to trust Him to meet your needs if you give to Him first? Then I urge you to begin giving now, because your fear will only dissolve when you replace it with faith. And you have the promise of God that He will care for you. You have nothing to wait for!

NOTES

To the Leader:

Spend some personal time studying and meditating on Ephesians 4; 1 Corinthians 12; and 2 Corinthians 8 and 9 this week. You don't need to present everything you learn from these passages in your group time, but your foundational knowledge will be invaluable to the group discussion.

During the Session

1. Ask why participants agree or disagree that it takes a village to raise a child. Ask why they agree or disagree that it takes a church to raise a Christian. OR Ask if participants like to watch animal programs on TV. Ask them to list what is common to most animal species. Ask: *Why do most animals stay in groups? What can Christians learn from the animal world?*

2. Read the first sentence of Day 1. Ask: *How do you think Jesus would respond to believers who declare they don't need the church?* Discuss the first activity of Day 1 (pp. 131-32). Comment that this explanation of Jesus' relationship with the church is in the middle of Paul's teachings about the family. The church is a family and plays a vital role in a believer's spiritual growth. Ask what other terms Paul used to describe the church in Ephesians 2:19-22 and what those terms emphasize. Ask: *Why would you pay money to go to a sporting event or movie when you can watch it at home?* Comment that there is a group dynamic that happens in a stadium or theater; some things are just better in a group! Guide the class to apply that principle to the church. Discuss the last activity in Day 1 (p. 132). Invite volunteers to share how the presence of others at church encourages them.

3. Ask learners to read 1 Corinthians 12:27 and share another term for the church. Invite participants to share why they like to look at infants' hands and feet. Ask: *Would it be a positive thing if those tiny hands and feet stayed little? Could they grow if they were severed from the body?* Acknowledge that is a gruesome image, but it might describe a fraction of the pain God feels when part of His Son's body, an individual believer, is unattached and not growing. Ask someone to read Ephesians 4:12-13. Remind them that hands and feet have to remain connected to the body so they can grow up and serve. Ask: *Which parts of the body are to serve and which are to be served?* Discuss the first activity of Day 2 (p. 133).

4. Ask: *How easy is it to distract or upset a child? Why?* Request that someone read Ephesians 4:13-14. Ask participants how they can know they

142

are growing toward the goal of becoming like Jesus. Explain that God wants us to mature to the point where we don't get distracted or blown over by life and its struggles. Discuss the second activity of Day 2. Talk about the importance of both truth and love and the church's role in providing both. Discuss the third activity of Day 2 (p. 134). Invite volunteers to share how the church has helped them grow.

5. Share: *It has been said that the last part of us to get saved is our checkbook.* Ask participants what they think that means. Ask what Dr. Evans meant by equating our giving with the lights on a car's dashboard. Talk about the giving statistics that indicate how your church looks "under the hood" (p. 136). Organize the class into two groups. Instruct Group 1 to read Acts 4:32-5:5 and Group 2 to read 2 Corinthians 8:1-5. Instruct both groups to name the givers, describe their priorities, and share what those priorities led them to do. Allow time for both groups to share. Discuss the first activity of Day 3. Ask someone to read the quotation in the margin of Day 3 (p. 136). Ask what blocked or encouraged the flow of God's grace in Ananias and the Macedonians.

6. Ask a volunteer to read 2 Corinthians 9:6. Explore why Paul used the analogy of a farmer to illustrate the concept of giving. Discuss the first activity of Day 4 (p. 138). Ask: *Does the promise in these verses just apply to money? Explain. What is the significance of God giving you more seed?* Ask participants what God expects of believers [tithe, offering]. Define both terms. Read Malachi 3:9-10 (p. 139). Ask how believers rob God. Discuss the second activity of Day 4. Discuss the meaning of curse and blessing.

7. Discuss the first activity of Day 5. Ask: *How can we be joyful about giving away our hard-earned money or precious time? According to 2 Corinthians 9:8, what does God promise to do when we give joyfully? Why does Christ want us to give?* Discuss the last activity of Day 5. Close the session in prayer.

Trials and Temptations

day One

Trials: The Test of Spiritual Growth

Trials are unscheduled, and usually unwelcome, interruptions in the normal pattern of life that always seem to come at the worst possible time. They may last for days, weeks, or even years, and the exact reason for them may never be completely clear to us. Trials can make us feel helpless, but we do have control over one vital element of a trial—how we respond to it.

Trials are indispensable to our spiritual growth. In fact, we cannot grow as we should without trials. Trials test our spiritual mettle and reveal what we are made of.

THE NECESSITY OF TRIALS TO OUR GROWTH

The Bible says the hard times we face in life are so important to our growth that we should actually welcome them. A trial comes as an adverse set of circumstances in our lives, either permitted or created by God, to develop us spiritually. Trials are not easy to handle. They hurt, and they can be costly. But God is behind our trials. And because God is in control, our trials have a good purpose, which is to grow and mature us spiritually.

Read James 1:2. What are Christians to do about trials?

❑ **Grit their teeth and bear them**
❑ **Find joy in them**
❑ **Find the quickest way out**

James 1:2 may be one of the hardest commands to obey in Scripture. We could handle it better if James told us to find joy in trials. But he said to respond to trials with "all joy." This means joy that is pure and unadulterated.

We tend to think of trials as the exception rather than the rule in life. But the reality is we are either in a trial right now, coming out of a trial, or heading toward our next one. We know that trials are inescapable because James used "when" and not "if" when it comes to encountering hard times.

The trials we encounter come in all varieties. Some are circumstantial in the sense that things aren't going right. We've all had those times when nothing seems to work out. We may also encounter physical, financial, relational, or emotional trials that knock us for a loop and interrupt our lives.

Whatever the color or shape of our trials, there is nowhere we can go to escape. Job said, "Man is born for trouble, as sparks fly upward" (Job 5:7). Jesus said, "In the world you have tribulation" (John 16:33).

Christians aren't the only people who have problems, but there is a great difference between the trials we experience as believers and the troubles of a non-Christian. For the Christian, there is no such thing as a purposeless trial. Every difficulty that comes our way as believers in Jesus Christ, no matter how severe or painful, has a reason attached to it. Trials are pain with a purpose, designed to launch us to the next spiritual level. God either sends us our trials directly or allows them to come—all for His reason.

> "Trials are pain with a purpose, designed to launch us to the next spiritual level. "
> —Tony Evans

THE REASON WE ENCOUNTER TRIALS

"Knowing that the testing of your faith produces endurance. And let endurance have its perfect result, so that you may be perfect and complete, lacking in nothing" (Jas. 1:3-4). The reason for our trials is to grow us into spiritual maturity. Trials are meant to refine us so that Christ may be reflected in us.

You may be saying, "I don't know. The trial I'm in right now feels like it's tearing me down instead of building me up." I'm not here to tell you the pain isn't real. The statement James makes about the purpose of trials is one we have to take by faith sometimes, but it is also a promise from the God whose Word never fails. We also have the testimony of saints who have emerged victoriously from countless trials over the centuries to tell us that God is faithful to bring good from even our hardest times.

Our trials are custom-made. Your trials have your name on them. Like a skilled tailor measuring a customer for a handmade suit that will fit perfectly, God the Holy Spirit is tailoring the trials we encounter to fit our spiritual needs.

James says that trials are "the testing of your faith." Trials call your faith to the witness stand, to see if we really believe what we affirmed when we sang that song and said "Amen" to the sermon last Sunday. We all want to grow, but we don't always want to take the test. We will never know what we can do spiritually until we experience the pressure of the battle.

The testing of our faith produces endurance. Endurance is the ability to hang in there until the trial is over and we have passed the test on our way to the next level of spiritual maturity. But this means we can't quit halfway through the test.

When we quit in the middle of a trial that is designed for our growth, it delays our advancement. Remember that God has His hand on the process and knows when to discontinue a trial because its purpose has been realized. In the meantime, He gives us great promises.

Write God's promises to you in each of these passages.

Isaiah 43:1-2 _____

Hebrews 12:10-11 _____

day Two

Enduring Trials Victoriously

WHAT IT TAKES TO ENDURE TRIALS VICTORIOUSLY

How can we endure these hard and often painful times so we can reap the blessing of spiritual maturity? James included several important factors that will help us handle trials to experience the victorious outcome God wants for us. These truths work no matter what the nature of any particular trial may be. The first thing that will help determine how we make it through a trial is how we look at it.

"Consider it all joy … when you encounter various trials" (Jas. 1:2). James doesn't say that trials are joyful things in themselves, but that we can be joyful in them because of what God is going to do through them. The joy James has in mind here is not circumstantial. Joy has to do with our internal well-being regardless of what is happening externally. Joy comes from knowing that God is using the trial to grow us.

Our example of patient endurance in trials is Jesus Himself. I love Hebrews 12:2, where the writer says of Jesus, "Who for the joy set before Him endured the cross." Joy and death on a cross are two concepts that don't go together in most people's minds. But Jesus was able to look past the cross because He knew glory awaited Him when He went back to His Father and delivered those whom He had redeemed.

Jesus still felt the agony of His trial. He prayed in the garden, "My Father, if it is possible, let this cup pass from Me" (Matt. 26:39). But the Bible also says He kept His eyes fixed on the outcome of the cross, which was redemption for us and resurrection and glory for Him.

The wisdom we need to handle our trials in a godly way comes from God alone. "If any of you lacks wisdom, let him ask of God, who gives to all generously and without reproach, and it will be given to him" (Jas. 1:5). This is not an invitation for us to quiz God about the why of our trials. That is information you and I may never know this side of heaven. Instead of asking why, we need to ask God, "How do You want to use this trial in my life to grow me spiritually, and what do You want me to do to cooperate with You in this trial so I can reap the benefits?"

But it's not enough to ask the right questions. We also need to ask with the right spirit. According to James 1:6-8, it is possible to ask God for wisdom and then mess around trying to decide whether we intend to obey Him or not. James calls this being "double-minded," and he is straight about the result: "That man ought not to expect that he will receive anything from the Lord, being a double-minded man, unstable in all his ways" (vv. 7–8). When you ask God for wisdom, your response needs to be, "Speak, Lord, for Your servant is listening."

I can't think of anything that will discourage you faster in the midst of a trial than trying to come at it from the human perspective. It's when you look at your trials from the eternal angle that you find your spirit is being renewed so you can press on to receive what God has waiting for you.

How to Win the Crown of Life

There is a great reward, a wonderful payoff, for being faithful in trials. James gave us examples of what a godly reaction to trials looks like in James 1:9-11. Read these verses prnted in the margin.

> "Joy comes from knowing that God is using the trial to grow us."
> —Tony Evans

> "The brother of humble circumstances is to glory in his high position; and the rich man is to glory in his humiliation, because like flowering grass he will pass away. For the sun rises with a scorching wind and withers the grass; and its flower falls off and the beauty of its appearance is destroyed; so too the rich man in the midst of his pursuits will fade away" (Jas. 1:9-11).

The first person mentioned is the poor man, or the person of "humble circumstances," who is told to "glory in his high position" (v. 9).

According to James 1:10-11, what lesson is the rich person to learn?

_____

Both the poor and the rich need to learn that God, and not anything else, is the source of their security. The poor can rejoice that they are rich in Christ, and the rich can rejoice that they have learned not to trust in the stock market and the retirement account. When these lessons are learned, spiritual growth takes place.

Read James 1:12 in your Bible. What is the payoff for faithfully seeing your test through to the end?

_____

When God gives you the crown of life, He is saying that you passed the test and now He is going to invade your circumstances with a new level of His power and glory that will make you feel more alive than you have ever felt in your life.

day *Three*

Temptation: The Battle of Spiritual Growth

Temptation comes in all shapes, sizes, colors, and forms. You and I will face temptation as long as we are alive. It is part of the spiritual battle we must wage if we are going to grow in the grace and knowledge of Jesus Christ.

THE REALITY OF TEMPTATION

According to James 1:13-14, the source of temptation

is not _____ but _____.

James 1:13-14 comes immediately after James's teaching about trials. The connection is important, because the same basic Greek word translated "trials" in James 1:2 is used in the verb form for "tempted" in verse 13. In fact, this is the case throughout the New Testament, which tells us that the same event can be either a trial or a temptation, depending on its purpose and how we respond to it.

The difference is that a trial is created or allowed by God to strengthen us in faith and advance our spiritual growth, while a temptation is a solicitation or enticement to evil that comes from the Devil and his demons. It's an invitation to disobey or rebel against God with the goal of stifling our spiritual growth and limiting our capacity to bring greater glory to God. A trial is designed to develop you; a temptation is designed to defeat you.

"A trial is designed to develop you; a temptation is designed to defeat you." —Tony Evans

Temptation is different from trials in its source, its purpose, and its outcome. Temptation is a work of the Enemy from beginning to end.

God does not tempt us, period. He tests and tries us so that we will endure and come out stronger, and He may even allow Satan to tempt us as part of our spiritual development. But any invitation to do wrong does not come from our God. God is perfectly holy and separate from sin. There is nothing in God that can respond to evil at all, and therefore He cannot be the source of bringing evil to anyone else. God is the source of everything good in our lives.

God won't cause you to sin—and the Devil can't make you sin. He can offer you a temptation and make it look inviting, but he cannot force you to sin. You have to cooperate. The Devil's power is influence and deception, not coercion.

Read Titus 2:11-12. What do you need to do when temptations come your way?

_____

What empowers you to do so?

day *Four*

The Progress and Source of Temptation

THE PROGRESS OF TEMPTATION

James 1:14-15 spells out clearly the way temptation progresses in a downward direction from an idea or a thought to an action and its consequences.

> **Read James 1:14-15. Identify the three steps in the progress of temptation:**
>
> 1. _____
>
> 2. _____
>
> 3. _____

Legitimate desires can be turned to illegitimate ends when they begin to dominate your thinking and actions.

Almost every temptation to sin is built off of a legitimate, God-given desire. If a temptation were not desirable to us in some way, we wouldn't be bothered by it. Satan knows how to take God's good gifts and mix them with deception and empty promises to entice us.

The next step downward in temptation is taken when the desire, fueled by Satan's enticement, leads us to disobedience. Notice that sin doesn't come until the temptation is accepted and acted upon. It's good news to know that it's not a sin to be tempted.

James tells us there is one more step in the progress of temptation as we move from desire to disobedience. That final step is death. Sin never stops until it brings about death—either eternal death for the unsaved or a rupture in the believer's fellowship with God, which is the essence of death.

We don't drop dead physically every time we sin, but a death occurs every time we sin. The result of yielding to temptation is the loss of fellowship with God and the stunting of spiritual growth, which is why confession of sin is so important. Nothing stunts spiritual growth faster than allowing temptation to breed sin and death.

THE SOURCE OF TEMPTATION

The Devil is the tempter. The Bible even calls him by that name in Matthew 4:3 when he came to Jesus in the wilderness to tempt Him. If God allowed Satan to tempt His own Son, He will allow Satan to tempt you and me.

The Devil is a master of temptation because he studies and knows you. The Devil knows your tendencies and weak spots. He knows what you are most likely to do and what temptation would have the best chance of success against you. The Devil is not all-knowing and all-powerful, so he cannot control us. But he can influence and plant thoughts and hit us where we are the weakest.

Read 1 Corinthians 10:13. What promise can you cling to when you are weak and tempted?

_____

When you're in the middle of a temptation, you may feel as if you can't handle it. But if a temptation reaches you, you can assume that it has passed through heaven's review and God knows it is within your ability to endure.

The way we know we can handle a temptation is that God provides with it "the way of escape." God's promise of escape doesn't mean we won't have to persevere and be faithful to Him. But it does mean that when God's purpose of victory over temptation and spiritual growth through it has been served, He will bring us out.

Our second enemy in temptation is the world. You and I have to live in this world, but we don't have to love it. Satan has a network that consists of people who carry out his will, whether they realize it or not. The world is hostile toward God because Satan is calling the shots, and therefore the world is hostile toward us. He tries to tantalize us with all the world has to offer, and too often believers are falling for it. Satan and the world don't mind you going to church on Sunday, as long as you leave God in church and don't make a big deal out of Him the rest of the week.

The third enemy we have to battle is our flesh, our inbred self-centeredness that gives the world and the Devil an entry point into our lives. The desires of the flesh won't go away. We will carry them throughout our lives. The Devil, the world, and the flesh are constantly calling us, trying to draw us away from God. But we have another system working for us that can intercept those calls before they become a problem.

day *Five*

How to Overcome Temptation

DRESSING FOR SPIRITUAL SUCCESS

The Bible tells us how to dress for spiritual success against Satan and his forces. The spiritual wardrobe we need is found in Ephesians 6. "Be strong in the Lord and in the strength of His might. Put on the full armor of God, so that you will be able to stand firm against the schemes of the Devil" (Eph. 6:10-11). Your strength is in the Lord and His might, not in the limited power of your human will. Our battle is supernatural, not natural, so we need the supernatural armor of God, which is available to us in Christ Jesus.

When we dress ourselves in God's armor, all we have to do is "stand firm" (vv. 11,13-14). In Christ the battle is already over and won. We're not fighting for victory, but from victory. Jesus won the battle over the world, the flesh, and the Devil.

I want to take you through the six pieces of God's armor described in Ephesians 6:14-17.

Read Ephesians 6:14-17. List in the margin the pieces of God's armor.

The first piece is the belt of truth (v. 14a). We have defined truth as a fixed, nonnegotiable standard to which everything else must adjust. God's Word is that standard. "Let God be found true, though every man be found a liar" (Rom. 3:4).

1. _____

_____

2. _____

_____

3. _____

_____

4. _____

_____

5. _____

_____

6. _____

_____

The second piece of God's armor is the breastplate of righteousness (Eph. 6:14b). The breastplate covers your heart, which in the Bible is the center of your consciousness. When you know God's truth, then your heart knows how to beat at the right rhythm. But once you let go of truth, God sets off a warning beeper inside that something is wrong—and it's not wise to ignore warning signals from your heart.

The third section of the believer's armor, the shoes of peace, confirms God's desire for us to be in fellowship with Him (v. 15a). This peace is the inner tranquility that comes from "the gospel of peace" through which we come into right standing with God.

The imagery of shoes suggests the need to stand firm. Shoes also mean that you are going somewhere. There is nothing static about the Christian life. Spiritual growth requires movement and development. Don't expect to hear from God if you remain frozen in the same spot all the time. When you move ahead for the Lord, He confirms the rightness of your decision by the peace He gives. You have a firm foundation under you.

The shield of faith is the fourth piece of armor and the first we are told to take up as we need it. The shield allows us "to extinguish all the flaming arrows of the evil one" (v. 16b). Satan's arrows, things like doubt and discouragement, are designed to distract us from the real battle and get us fighting the fires started by the arrows.

If you're under attack and need your shield, you are also going to need the helmet of salvation (v. 17a). A helmet protects your brain, or mind, which for the Christian has to do with your new identity or who you are in Christ—a blood bought, totally forgiven, absolutely redeemed, heaven-bound child of God.

The sixth and last piece of armor is the sword of the Spirit, "which is the word of God" (v. 17b). This refers to our use of God's Word to defeat Satan in battle, using the right Scripture at the right time to deal with the problem at hand. The Devil can out-argue and out-debate us, but he has no answer for the Word of God.

According to Ephesians 6:18, how do we put on the armor of God?

Praying in the power of the Spirit clothes us for spiritual warfare, which is what we are talking about. I encourage you to pray specifically at the start of every day, asking God to clothe you with each piece of His armor you are supposed to wear at all times and to enable you to take up the pieces of armor you need as the occasion demands. Don't go out for the day spiritually underdressed.

PUTTING ON JESUS

Jesus is our armor. When we talk about putting on our armor, we are really talking about putting on Christ. That's why the Bible commands us, "Put on the Lord Jesus Christ, and make no provision for the flesh in regard to its lusts" (Rom. 13:14). Paul mentioned the flesh because it is the only one of our three enemies we can do something about. We can't keep the Devil from being himself and the world from throwing its enticements at us, but we don't have to respond to them in our flesh.

Let me tell you what putting on Jesus will do for you. Hebrews 2:18 says that Jesus was tempted as we are tempted so that He can deliver us when we are tempted. What you need to do is keep your eyes fixed on Jesus (see Heb. 12:2). If you keep your eyes on Jesus Christ, it won't matter what Satan throws your way. Every now and then you may want to go for it, but if you keep your eyes on Jesus and listen for His voice alone, you can be victorious over anything.

> "If you keep your eyes on Jesus and listen for His voice alone, you can be victorious over anything." —Tony Evans

Read James 4:7 and 1 John 4:4. When faced with temptation what is:

Your responsibility?_____

God's promise?_____

To the Leader:

Recruit someone to plan several fellowship activites for your class. Make every effort to keep participants active and involved in Bible study and fellowship through the summer months.

Before the Session

Ask volunteers to be prepared to read John 14:6; 1 Corinthians 1:30; Ephesians 2:14; Hebrews 12:2; 1 John 4:14; and John 1:1. (Step 7)

During the Session

1. Ask: *What situations cause you to ask, "What is the purpose of this?" Could you handle committee meetings or slow traffic better if you knew there was a purpose behind them? Why?* OR Encourage participants to list activities that are physically and emotionally demanding [ball practices, basic training, marathons, medical internships]. Ask: *What is the purpose of these difficult activities?* FOR EITHER OPTION Read Deuteronomy 8:2. Ask what God's purpose was in allowing His children to face hardships. Explain that God still allows His children to face trials and temptations to grow them up.

2. Challenge the class to read James 1:2-8 and identify the right attitude, right ambition, and right approach to trials, using the material in Days 1 and 2 as an aid. [Samples: attitude—joy; ambition—to develop complete perseverance which leads to maturity; approach—ask for wisdom with unwavering faith.] Option: Instruct three groups to identify the right attitude, ambition, and approach in James 1:2-8; 2 Corinthians 4:16-18; and 1 Peter 1:5-9. Discuss the final activity of Day 1 (p. 146).

3. Invite a volunteer to read James 1:9-11. Ask: *How can both being in need and having wealth test our faith?* Ask participants to follow along in their Bibles as you read Deuteronomy 8:2-5,10-15. Discuss how the Israelites faced the same tests of need and wealth. Debate whether having too little or too much is a greater test of faithfulness. Inquire: *What lessons does God want His children to learn in either situation?* Discuss the final activity of Day 2 (p. 148). Ask: *Do you think the crown of life is something we will enjoy only in heaven or is it for the present as well? Explain.*

4. Request that someone read James 1:13. Guide the class to explore the difference between trials and temptations. Ask what trial God gave Adam and Eve in Genesis 2:16-17 and how they could have matured

through that trial. Ask how Satan turned that trial into a temptation in Genesis 3. Discuss: *Why might God ordain the trial of financial hardship in your life? How might Satan turn that trial into a temptation? How valid is the excuse "the Devil made me do it"? Why?* Discuss the final activity of Day 3 (pp. 149-50). Ask: *Why would saying no to temptation lead to spiritual growth?* Remind participants that we grow when God's grace flows.

5. Complete the first activity of Day 4. Lead the class to describe how material greed and physical lust would follow this progression. Identify the types of death that occur when people give in to temptation. Explain that the terrorist organization of al Qaeda with its evil leader, evil system, and evil desires illustrates the battle believers face daily. Ask why the Devil is the master of temptation. Request that someone read 1 John 2:15-16. Inquire: *What does the world have to offer?* Give examples of how believers fall for what the world offers. Discuss the second activity of Day 4 (p. 151).

6. Explain that God has promised we can win the battle but that doesn't mean the battle is going to be easy. Ask someone to read Ephesians 6:10-13. Ask why we need God's strength. Share that just as soldiers wouldn't attempt to fight a 21st century war with 15th century weapons, so believers must not try to fight a supernatural war with human weapons. Guide the class to name human weapons believers use to try to fight temptation. To discover God's weapons for this battle, use Dr. Evans's comments to explore each piece of armor. Discuss the second activity of Day 5 (p. 153).

7. Ask the first volunteer you enlisted to read John 14:6. Ask: *What is the belt of truth we are to put on?* Ask that same question about each piece of the armor in Ephesians 6 after the other volunteers read their verses. Ask: *What are we really putting on when we put on this spiritual armor?* (see Rom. 13:14). *How can that give you victory over temptation?* Discuss the final activity of Day 5.

Calling, Obedience, and Maturity

day One

Calling: The Ministry of Spiritual Growth

Finding and living out your calling as a believer is an important step of spiritual growth. True fulfillment is discovering the reason God put you on earth in the first place.

THE MEANING OF A CALLING

Your calling is the customized life purpose that God has shaped, fashioned, and equipped for you. One reason God wants you to grow in your faith is so that you will be able to maximize your calling, both for your joy and fulfillment and for His glory.

God is a God of purpose. Everything in the universe He created has a purpose behind it, and He made us with that same desire and drive to find a purpose for our existence. This desire in us reflects God's orderly nature, which is revealed in Genesis 1 as He assigned each portion of the creation its designated purpose. Light was given to dispel the darkness and keep it in its place. The sun was created to "govern" or give light during the day, and the moon was to "govern" the night (Gen. 1:16).

Too many of us are like singers trying to perform outside their range—straining and getting off-key because we are not fulfilling our divinely ordained purpose. Acts 13:36 makes a very significant statement about King David of Israel: "For David, after he had served the purpose of God in his own generation, fell asleep, and was laid among his fathers." There is no greater epitaph that could be put over our lives than to say we fulfilled God's purpose in our generation.

" 'For I know the plans that I have for you,' declares the LORD, 'plans for welfare and not for calamity to give you a future and a hope' " (Jer. 29:11).

"For we are His workmanship, created in Christ Jesus for good works, which God prepared beforehand so that we would walk in them" (Eph. 2:10).

THE CHARACTER OF YOUR CALLING

God has a calling tailor-made for you. It's your salvation, not someone else's. In the same way that you have unique fingerprints and DNA, you have a unique calling.

God is so intentional in fashioning a unique purpose for each of His children that the Holy Spirit has equipped every believer with what the Bible calls a spiritual gift, or a divine enablement for service (see 1 Cor. 12:7,11).

A spiritual gift is not simply a human talent or ability. A gift is more than a talent, because a gift is something the Spirit of God uses to promote the purposes and glory of God through your life. Spiritual gifts are given by the Holy Spirit to enable you to fulfill your calling from God and further His program on earth.

Do you know what God has called you to do? Do you know how God has gifted you? If so, how are you using your giftedness for God's glory?

When you discover God's calling, you won't have to force yourself to fit anywhere. The Bible says that God has placed each part of Christ's body exactly where He wants it to be (see 1 Cor. 12:18). There is tremendous satisfaction in finding that place and knowing this is where God called you to be.

Read Psalm 138:8. Write this verse in your own words as a prayer that you will fulfill the unique purpose for which God created you.

_____

_____

> "To each one is given the manifestation of the Spirit for the common good. ... But one and the same Spirit works all these things, distributing to each one individually just as He wills (1 Cor. 12:7,11).

day *Two*

Your Calling and Success

THE PROPER TIME FOR YOUR CALLING

The Holy Spirit called out Barnabas and Saul, or Paul, by name in the context of the church's corporate worship. The Holy Spirit still speaks to believers today as we participate in the body of Christ. God's call on individuals is for the benefit of the body. The church also acts as the confirming agent for the calling of individual believers. The best place to discover your call is at church.

One reason so many believers are missing their calling is that they aren't in the place where God can speak to them objectively through His Word and subjectively through His Spirit, confirmed by His people and circumstances. They are on the sidelines waiting for something to happen.

As you grow in the Word, in faith, and in service, you give God a growing target to hit. Don't put off serving the Lord until you find your call. It was not until Moses turned aside to investigate the burning bush that he heard God's explicit purpose for him.

THE ELEMENTS OF YOUR CALLING

God uses your circumstances to prepare you for your calling. It was at the burning bush that God revealed to Moses his calling as Israel's deliverer. None of Moses' 80 years of training was wasted.

Many of us don't know the Spirit's voice. We've never heard Him call our names. I'm talking about the reality of God the Holy Spirit speaking to your heart and clearly communicating with you what He wants you to do.

Another important element in your calling is passion—a burning desire or fire in your heart to do a particular work for God's glory. A God-given passion for your calling motivates and compels you. It's the fire that cannot be quenched. When He sets your heart ablaze, you begin to see things you never saw before and you get excited about them. The Holy Spirit stands ready to inflame your heart for a calling that is from Him.

A DEFINITION OF TRUE SUCCESS

When you define success in terms of God's calling, the standard changes. True success is not what you have done compared to what others have done but what you have done compared to what you were supposed to do. Jesus was successful because He completed the work His Father sent Him to do (see John 17:4). Paul was successful because he finished his race (see 2 Tim. 4:5-8).

We will not be truly successful until we are using our gifts to fulfill our calling. One thing that concerns me as a pastor is seeing Christians use their abilities in their profession but not for the kingdom.

"True success is not what you have done compared to what others have done but what you have done compared to what you were supposed to do."
—Tony Evans

Read 1 Corinthians 12:7. Why does the Holy Spirit give you gifts?

_____

Have you been using your gifts and talents for
❑ **your own good   or   ❑ the good of Christ's body?**

Unless and until we are using our gifts to advance God's kingdom, we will not enjoy His divine sense of calling and satisfaction. Your calling is the place where you will experience the abundant life Jesus promised.

What impact are you making for the kingdom of God? What time and talent and energy are you devoting to your call? How are you using the gifts God bestowed on you to carry out His program?

When you discover your calling, you'll know it, because you will be more alive than you ever were before. God's grace will have set you free to become all you were created to be.

Describe your understanding of your calling. If you have not yet discovered your calling, write a prayer asking the Holy Spirit to show you the gifts God has given you and the ways He wants to use them.

_____

_____

day *Three*

Obedience: The Response of Spiritual Growth

The way we respond to the expectations God places upon us as His children is another vital component in our spiritual growth. Obedience to God's will as revealed in the Scripture is the standard, and any Christian who wants to please God and grow will seek to be obedient.

A NEW DEFINITION OF OBEDIENCE

The connection between the new nature that God put within us at salvation and our obedience to Him is vital. When He made us new creations in Christ, He also gave us the internal desire to obey His law by walking in His ways.

Most of us equate obedience with the "do it or else" approach. The Bible gives us a better definition of obedience, which is doing what you really want to do deep down inside.

As Christians, most of us do not look at obedience as the activation and cultivation of something that is already present within us. We consider obedience a responsibility we have to manufacture, not something we already have the "want to" to perform.

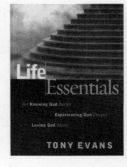

It should be pleasurable for us to obey, both because God is pleased by our obedience and because we are pleased knowing that we have made Him happy. If we treat obedience as nothing more than outward compliance divorced from anything that's happening on the inside, then we are not experiencing any joy in what we are doing.

Jesus said, "Come to Me, all who are weary and heavy-laden, and I will give you rest. Take My yoke upon you and learn from Me, for I am gentle and humble in heart, and you will find rest for your souls. For My yoke is easy and My burden is light" (Matt. 11:28-30).

Does Jesus have a yoke for us to bear that includes obedience? Absolutely. Does He intend it to be a wearying, tiring load of responsibility that is so heavy we can barely manage it? Absolutely not. If your load is too heavy for you, bring it to Jesus and let Him show you the joy of following and obeying Him.

OBEDIENCE, THE OVERFLOW OF LOVE

Read John 14:23-24 and 1 John 5:3. What proves you love God?

_____

Jesus said obedience is the proof of love. We prove our love for God by obeying Him. Obedience is the natural overflow of love. And when you love someone, obedience is not a burdensome thing. The formula is simple. If we love Jesus, the desire to obey will be there. If we will bask in God's perfect love, we won't have any problem doing the things that He asks us to do.

Does your level of obedience prove you have a greater love for ❏ God or ❏ yourself?

Removing Hindrances to Obedience

A BIBLICAL PATTERN FOR OBEDIENCE
When we're looking for practical application of biblical truth, we often wind up in the Book of James. Here are some ways we can respond to God's Word.

Seek God's Mind at All Times
"Everyone must be quick to hear, slow to speak and slow to anger; for the anger of man does not achieve the righteousness of God" (Jas. 1:19-20). James is talking about being quick to hear God's Word. The first question we need to ask in any situation is, *What does God say about this in His Word? What is His mind on this?*

James says you also need to be slow in your response. When you learn what God says, don't react in the flesh because your flesh does not want to obey God. Getting angry doesn't do any good either, because you aren't going to change God's mind, and when it's all over, you still need to obey.

Remove Hindrances to Obeying
"Putting aside all filthiness and all that remains of wickedness, in humility receive the word implanted, which is able to save your souls" (Jas. 1:21). The hindrances James mentions act like calluses on our hearts and keep us from obeying the Lord. We need to remove these so the soft flesh of the new nature can be revealed, which is where the "want to" for obeying God is located. Heartfelt confession removes these hindrances and prepares the way for the Holy Spirit to apply God's Word to our lives.

See Yourself in the Word

The goal of seeing ourselves in God's Word is to become "doers of the word, and not merely hearers who delude themselves" (v. 22). The opposite of someone who obeys the Word is the person described in verses 23–24: "For if anyone is a hearer of the word and not a doer, he is like a man who looks at his natural face in a mirror; for once he has looked at himself and gone away, he has immediately forgotten what kind of person he was."

The point is the difference between taking a quick glance at yourself and hanging out in front of the mirror until you have fully seen who you are. When we read God's Word or hear it taught or preached, the Holy Spirit uses it to hold up a mirror before us. A doer of the Word or a Christian who wants to grow not only wants to read the Bible or hear it preached. He wants to see himself in the Bible so he can make whatever adjustments are necessary.

Continue to Abide in the Word

Read James 1:25 printed in the margin. List three things believers are to do with God's Word.

1. _____

2. _____

3. _____

"One who looks intently at the perfect law, the law of liberty, and abides by it, not having become a forgetful hearer but an effectual doer, this man will be blessed in what he does" (Jas. 1:25).

The person God blesses is the one who "abides" in His Word. *Abide* means to hang out, to stick around. When you look into the mirror of Scripture, you not only see yourself, but you see what God wants you to become. When you look intently into the Word in order to find out what God wants from you, you are on your way to an exciting adventure with Christ.

When we look into the Word, we behold the glory of God. And since bringing God glory is our primary purpose for being on earth, He wants to change us so as to reflect His glory more and more.

But this can't happen if we are in the habit of just grabbing a Bible verse here and there or quickly skimming through a passage. If your prayer in coming to the Word is, "God, show me how I can glorify You today through my obedience to You," then you are going to hang out with the Word until the Holy Spirit connects with your spirit and brings about a change within you. That's when spiritual growth breaks out.

Maturity: The Goal of Spiritual Growth

We can define spiritual maturity as the ability to consistently view and live life from the perspective of the Spirit rather than the flesh, with the result that we maximize our God-given capacity to bring Him glory.

This is something we will be pursuing and living out all of our lives, but spiritual growth does have a definable goal called maturity that we need to be moving toward. And there are definable stages along the way.

THREE LEVELS OF SPIRITUAL DEVELOPMENT

First John 1 addresses three groups of Christians who represent three levels or stages of spiritual growth in the process of our becoming more like Jesus Christ and bringing God greater glory. These stages correspond to the childhood, adolescence or teenage years, and adulthood of physical life.

The Stage of Spiritual Childhood

People at this stage of spiritual growth are still coming to grips with the exciting fact that Jesus Christ has forgiven all their sins and they have been rescued from judgment and eternal death.

It's basic ABC spiritual truth, which is all new Christians can handle at this early stage. They are limited in their understanding, and there is nothing wrong with that if they are truly new to the faith.

"I am writing to you, little children, because your sins have been forgiven you for His name's sake. ... I have written to you, children, because you know the Father" (1 John 2:12,13).

Baby Christians need someone to feed them and help them make their way along in the spiritual life. Spiritual infancy is also marked by instability. For baby Christians, stability or the lack thereof is dictated by their circumstances. If things are fine, so are they. But when times get tough, they are far from fine. They have not yet made the crucial connection between trials and spiritual development. Spiritual children are more dependent on the ministry and input of others than more mature Christians are.

Read 1 Peter 2:2. If you are a baby Christian, what do you need to make sure you are doing?

_____

Becoming a Spiritual Young Person

This period of life is marked by conflict and the need to become spiritually strong and learn how to overcome the Devil. At this stage a young person is coming to grips with the realities of the Christian life and is often engaged in real combat with the Devil. These are the years of the Christian life when we first learn how to use the sword of the Spirit, God's Word, to counter the attacks of the Enemy.

While young Christians are learning to be strong and overcome the Devil with the Word of God, they still need the support and guidance of mature Christians to help them handle conflicts, whether they think so or not. Adolescent Christians want to move forward in these experiences, and they often feel they can take on the world, the flesh, and the Devil all by themselves. But they need help and direction to become strong.

> "I am writing to you, young men, because you have overcome the evil one. ... I have written to you, young men, because you are strong, and the word of God abides in you, and you have overcome the evil one" (1 John 2:13,14).

Becoming a Mature Adult

Read 1 John 2:13 in the margin. What identifies a mature Christian?

_____

> "I am writing to you, fathers, because you know Him who has been from the beginning" (1 John 2:13).

The mature believer knows God in a depth of intimacy that has been developing over time. The mature believer is tapping into a deeper understanding of God and His eternal nature, a process that suggests the passage of time.

A mature believer still needs to grow in Christlikeness, because that's a lifetime job. And there are still battles with the Enemy to fight and win. But a mature Christian's life has a quality of depth about it that can only be gained by going through the process of growing and battling.

How do you know when you know God in such an intimate way? The short answer is that your spirit is able to commune with God at such a deep level that you pick up signals other folk miss.

Your spirit is the deepest part of your being, and it gives you the ability to connect with God. You relate to the world through your body and to yourself through your soul, but you relate to God and other people through your spirit.

A growing and developing Christian who has been communing with the Lord for many years enters a higher level of spiritual awareness. In other words, mature Christians see things that the human eye can't see.

165

They hear things the most acute hearing on earth cannot detect. And they have thoughts they did not originate on their own because the Holy Spirit is helping them think God's thoughts. You will know you are spiritually mature when God lets you pick up on spiritual truths and insights from His Word that go far beyond what someone told you or what you heard in a sermon.

It has to do with the intimacy of your relationship with God. Spiritually mature Christians have a passion to pursue and know God, and they aren't satisfied until they are in intimate fellowship with Him.

> "It has to do with the intimacy of your relationship with God. Spiritually mature Christians have a passion to pursue and know God, and they aren't satisfied until they are in intimate fellowship with Him." —Tony Evans

THE EVIDENCE OF YOUR INTIMACY WITH GOD

As you grow in the grace and knowledge of Christ, your growth will manifest itself first to you and then to others. God will increasingly make Himself real to you, and your joy will be full.

My prayer for you is that you will grow into such close communion of heart and mind with God that whenever you hear or read His Word, it will have your name on it. And when you pray, your spirit will discern the Spirit of God revealing the mind and heart of God to you.

If you want to know God, then everything you do must have that as its driving goal. How quickly and solidly you grow depends on how hungry you are for growth. The diligence with which you use your time to pursue God will determine the speed at which you arrive at your destination of maturity.

> "Wherever you are on your journey with Christ, the best place to start growing is right where you are." —Tony Evans

Wherever you are on your journey with Christ, the best place to start growing is right where you are. You can't go back to yesterday, but today is a brand-new day to draw close to the Lord and hear from Him.

> "Therefore … let us press on to maturity" (Heb. 6:1).

At what stage of spiritual development are you? Circle your answer.

Childhood　　　　**Adolescence**　　　　**Mature Adult**

Write a prayer expressing your desire and commitment to "press on to maturity."

_____

_____

_____

_____

To the Leader:

Search "spiritual gifts" on *www.lifeway.com* for books, Bible studies, sermon outlines, teaching plans, and tools to download that you can recommend to your participants if they would like further help discerning and developing their spiritual gifts.

Before the Session

Prepare a handout with these questions: How are God's gifts part of His unique calling? What is the purpose of these gifts? How can these gifts be used to serve yourself? others? How can you use God's gifts to fulfill your calling? (Step 2)

During the Session

1. Ask: *Do you think every person has a specific purpose for living? What percentage of people would you say know the reason God put them on this earth? What do you think would happen to our spiritual growth if we knew our purpose for existing? Why?* OR Brainstorm names of plotless TV shows where the characters meander around with little purpose. Ask why group members think those programs are popular. Explain that God doesn't desire us to lead "Seinfeld" lives with no plot or purpose; we need to find our divinely-ordained reason for being.

2. Ask the class what Dr. Evans means by "calling." Invite two volunteers to read the Scriptures in the margin of Day 1 (pp. 157-58). Ask: *What can we know for sure about God's purpose for us?* Share that although God's general calling for all believers is to do good works, He also has a calling unique to each person and has given gifts to equip that calling. Distribute the handout. Instruct half the class to complete the handout using 1 Corinthians 12:7-11 and the other half to do the same with 1 Peter 4:10-11. Invite participants to share what they discover. Discuss the difference between a spiritual gift and a talent and how some believers might be using their gift as a personal talent. Encourage participants to use their gifts for God's glory so they can experience spiritual growth.

3. Ask a volunteer to read Acts 13:1-2. Ask where Paul and Barnabas received their calling as missionaries. Discuss why faithful church involvement is essential in discovering your calling. Ask what else God uses besides His Word and other believers to reveal His calling and prepare us to carry it out. Ask participants about Moses' unique calling. Challenge them to recall circumstances in Moses' life that led up to and

prepared him for that calling. (They may scan Exodus 1–2 if necessary.) Remind participants that Moses received this call when he was 80—it's never too late to receive and fulfill your calling. Discuss the role of passion in discovering and fulfilling your calling. Explore how believers can discover the things of God about which they are passionate.

4. Ask someone to read John 21:18-22. Ask what Jesus says to us when we compare our calling with others. Invite someone to read the quotation in the margin of Day 2 (p. 159). Explore how that statement is both liberating and challenging. Remind participants that God wants them to know their unique calling and they can discover that calling through staying power—1. Stay in the Word; 2. Stay on your knees; 3. Stay passionate about God's kingdom instead of yourself; 4. Stay busy doing what you know to do and God will reveal the next step.

5. Invite volunteers to describe a time they did something that really pleased a loved one. Ask: *What did it cost you? What was the payoff for you? Would it have been as pleasurable for you if you had been forced to do this thing for your loved one?* Explain that God has expectations of us and the way we respond to those expectations will influence our spiritual growth and fulfillment in life. Discuss different ways believers respond to God's expectations. Ask how Dr. Evans's description of obedience in Day 3 (p. 161) compares with what they always felt about obedience. Discuss the first activity in Day 3 (p. 161). Read Philippians 2:13. Discuss what God gives believers in regard to obedience.

6. Ask someone to read James 1:19-25. Ask the class to identify the practical pattern for obedience outlined in these verses and explain how it leads to spiritual growth. Direct the class to state specific ways believers can use this pattern to be obedient to God when they: 1. Have difficulty getting along with someone; 2. Need to get rid of a negative habit or attitude.

7. Request that participants read 1 John 2:12-14. Lead them to identify and discuss the three levels of spiritual development. Invite volunteers to share how this study has moved them toward spiritual maturity. Close in prayer that each participant will commit to press on to maturity.

8. Announce that next Sunday the class will begin a new study of Ray Stedman's *Authentic Christianity*. Ask learners to call absent members and encourage them to be present for the new lessons from the beginning.